S0-BNI-057

ELIJAH MUHAMMAD

BP
223
.Z8
E45
1990

Halasa, Malu.

Elijah Muhammad.

$7.95

DATE			

CHICAGO PUBLIC LIBRARY
VODAK EAST SIDE BRANCH
3710 E. 106TH STREET
CHICAGO, IL 60617

BAKER & TAYLOR BOOKS

ELIJAH MUHAMMAD

⋯

Malu Halasa

Senior Consulting Editor
Nathan Irvin Huggins
Director
W.E.B. Du Bois Institute for Afro-American Research
Harvard University

CHELSEA HOUSE PUBLISHERS
New York   Philadelphia

Chelsea House Publishers
Editor-in-Chief   Nancy Toff
Executive Editor   Remmel T. Nunn
Managing Editor   Karyn Gullen Browne
Copy Chief   Juliann Barbato
Picture Editor   Adrian G. Allen
Art Director   Maria Epes
Manufacturing Manager   Gerald Levine

Black Americans of Achievement
Senior Editor   Richard Rennert

Staff for ELIJAH MUHAMMAD
Associate Editor   Kate Barrett
Copy Editor   Michael Goodman
Deputy Copy Chief   Mark Rifkin
Editorial Assistant   Leigh Hope Wood
Picture Researcher   Patricia Burns
Assistant Art Director   Loraine Machlin
Designer   Ghila Krajzman
Production Manager   Joseph Romano
Production Coordinator   Marie Claire Cebrián
Cover Illustration   Alan J. Nahigian

Copyright © 1990 by Chelsea House Publishers, a division of
Main Line Book Co. All rights reserved. Printed and bound in
the United States of America.

7   9   8

Library of Congress Cataloging-in-Publication Data

Halasa, Malu.
  Elijah Muhammad : religious leader/Malu Halasa.
    p.   cm.—(Black Americans of Achievement)
  Summary: A biography of a leader of the Black Muslim movement,
which combined religious beliefs with strong social protest.
  ISBN 1-55546-602-8
        0-7910-0246-2 (pbk.)
  1. Elijah Muhammad, 1897–1975—Juvenile literature.   2. Black
Muslims—Biography—Juvenile literature.   [1. Elijah Muhammad,
1897–1975.   2. Muslims, Black.   3. Afro-Americans—Biography.]
I. Title.   II. Series.
BP223.Z8E45   1990
297'.87'092—dc20   89-29883
[B]   CIP
[92]   AC

Frontispiece: A portrait of Elijah Muhammad provides the backdrop for a convention attended by his son Wallace (center) and other Black Muslims.

R00974 05275

CONTENTS

CHICAGO PUBLIC LIBRARY
EAST SIDE BRANCH
10542 S. EWING AVE. 60617

BLACK AMERICANS OF ACHIEVEMENT

RALPH ABERNATHY
civil rights leader

MUHAMMAD ALI
heavyweight champion

RICHARD ALLEN
religious leader and social activist

LOUIS ARMSTRONG
musician

ARTHUR ASHE
tennis great

JOSEPHINE BAKER
entertainer

JAMES BALDWIN
author

BENJAMIN BANNEKER
scientist and mathematician

AMIRI BARAKA
poet and playwright

COUNT BASIE
bandleader and composer

ROMARE BEARDEN
artist

JAMES BECKWOURTH
frontiersman

MARY McLEOD
BETHUNE
educator

BLANCHE BRUCE
politician

RALPH BUNCHE
diplomat

GEORGE WASHINGTON
CARVER
botanist

CHARLES CHESNUTT
author

BILL COSBY
entertainer

PAUL CUFFE
merchant and abolitionist

FATHER DIVINE
religious leader

FREDERICK DOUGLASS
abolitionist editor

CHARLES DREW
physician

W.E.B. DU BOIS
scholar and activist

PAUL LAURENCE DUNBAR
poet

KATHERINE DUNHAM
dancer and choreographer

MARIAN WRIGHT EDELMAN
civil rights leader and lawyer

DUKE ELLINGTON
bandleader and composer

RALPH ELLISON
author

JULIUS ERVING
basketball great

JAMES FARMER
civil rights leader

ELLA FITZGERALD
singer

MARCUS GARVEY
black-nationalist leader

DIZZY GILLESPIE
musician

PRINCE HALL
social reformer

W. C. HANDY
father of the blues

WILLIAM HASTIE
educator and politician

MATTHEW HENSON
explorer

CHESTER HIMES
author

BILLIE HOLIDAY
singer

JOHN HOPE
educator

LENA HORNE
entertainer

LANGSTON HUGHES
poet

ZORA NEALE HURSTON
author

JESSE JACKSON
civil rights leader and politician

JACK JOHNSON
heavyweight champion

JAMES WELDON JOHNSON
author

SCOTT JOPLIN
composer

BARBARA JORDAN
politician

MARTIN LUTHER KING, JR.
civil rights leader

ALAIN LOCKE
scholar and educator

JOE LOUIS
heavyweight champion

RONALD McNAIR
astronaut

MALCOLM X
militant black leader

THURGOOD MARSHALL
Supreme Court justice

ELIJAH MUHAMMAD
religious leader

JESSE OWENS
champion athlete

CHARLIE PARKER
musician

GORDON PARKS
photographer

SIDNEY POITIER
actor

ADAM CLAYTON POWELL, JR.
political leader

LEONTYNE PRICE
opera singer

A. PHILIP RANDOLPH
labor leader

PAUL ROBESON
singer and actor

JACKIE ROBINSON
baseball great

BILL RUSSELL
basketball great

JOHN RUSSWURM
publisher

SOJOURNER TRUTH
antislavery activist

HARRIET TUBMAN
antislavery activist

NAT TURNER
slave revolt leader

DENMARK VESEY
slave revolt leader

MADAM C. J. WALKER
entrepreneur

BOOKER T. WASHINGTON
educator

HAROLD WASHINGTON
politician

WALTER WHITE
civil rights leader and author

RICHARD WRIGHT
author

ON
ACHIEVEMENT

————— ❧ —————

Coretta Scott King

BEFORE YOU BEGIN this book, I hope you will ask yourself what the word *excellence* means to you. I think that it's a question we should all ask and keep asking as we grow older and change. Because the truest answer to it should never change. When you think of excellence, perhaps you think of success at work; or of becoming wealthy; or meeting the right person, getting married, and having a good family life.

Those important goals are worth striving for, but there is a better way to look at excellence. As Martin Luther King, Jr., said in one of his last sermons, "I want you to be first in love. I want you to be first in moral excellence. I want you to be first in generosity. If you want to be important, wonderful. If you want to be great, wonderful. But recognize that he who is greatest among you shall be your servant."

My husband, Martin Luther King, Jr., knew that the true meaning of achievement is service. When I met him, in 1952, he was already ordained as a Baptist preacher and was working toward a doctoral degree at Boston University. I was studying at the New England Conservatory and dreamed of accomplishments in music. We married a year later, and after I graduated the following year we moved to Montgomery, Alabama. We didn't know it then, but our notions of achievement were about to undergo a dramatic change.

You may have read or heard about what happened next. What began with the boycott of a local bus line grew into a national movement, and by the time he was assassinated in 1968 my husband had fashioned a black movement powerful enough to shatter forever the practice of racial segregation. What you may not have read about is where he got his method for resisting injustice without compromising his religious beliefs.

He adopted the strategy of nonviolence from a man of a different race, who lived in a distant country, and even practiced a different religion. The man was Mahatma Gandhi, the great leader of India, who devoted his life to serving humanity in the spirit of love and nonviolence. It was in these principles that Martin discovered his method for social reform. More than anything else, those two principles were the key to his achievements.

This book is about black Americans who served society through the excellence of their achievements. It forms a part of the rich history of black men and women in America—a history of stunning accomplishments in every field of human endeavor, from literature and art to science, industry, education, diplomacy, athletics, jurisprudence, even polar exploration.

Not all of the people in this history had the same ideals, but I think you will find something that all of them have in common. Like Martin Luther King, Jr., they all decided to become "drum majors" and serve humanity. In that principle—whether it was expressed in books, inventions, or song—they found something outside themselves to use as a goal and a guide. Something that showed them a way to serve others, instead of living only for themselves.

Reading the stories of these courageous men and women not only helps us discover the principles that we will use to guide our own lives but also teaches us about our black heritage and about America itself. It is crucial for us to know the heroes and heroines of our history and to realize that the price we paid in our struggle for equality in America was dear. But we must also understand that we have gotten as far as we have partly because America's democratic system and ideals made it possible.

We are still struggling with racism and prejudice. But the great men and women in this series are a tribute to the spirit of our democratic ideals and the system in which they have flourished. And that makes their stories special and worth knowing. ◖◗

ELIJAH MUHAMMAD

1

"IN THE WILDERNESS OF NORTH AMERICA"

❧

B Y THE BEGINNING of 1963, preparations were already under way for a massive civil rights march to be held that August in Washington, D.C. A. Philip Randolph, who had organized America's first trade union for blacks nearly 40 years earlier, conceived the plan for the protest. But it was Bayard Rustin, a chief aide to the Reverend Martin Luther King, Jr., and a cofounder of an influential antidiscrimination organization, the Southern Christian Leadership Conference (SCLC), who enlarged the purpose of the demonstration. Rustin cajoled virtually every prominent civil rights leader and organization into participating because he knew that a huge, celebrity-studded March on Washington for Jobs and Freedom would bring the social and economic plight of black Americans to the attention of the public.

Anxious to win racial equality, Rustin, King, the Reverend Ralph Abernathy, and other moderate blacks had been staging nonviolent acts of social protest—including sit-ins, interstate bus rides, and voter registration drives—since the mid-1950s. "In a multiracial society no group can make it alone," King counseled his supporters. "To succeed in a pluralistic society, and an often hostile one at that, the Negro

Muhammad, surrounded by the Nation of Islam's paramilitary body, the Fruit of Islam, addresses his followers at an annual convention. The complete inscription on the banner (at top) is THERE IS NO GOD BUT ALLAH. MUHAMMAD IS HIS APOSTLE.

11

obviously needs organized strength, but that strength will only be effective when it is consolidated through constructive alliances with the [white] majority." Total integration seemed the sole way to wipe out the humiliating system of legalized segregation that the United States had maintained for the past 100 years.

Yet the nonviolent tactics and integrationist policies favored by most civil rights leaders had its opponents among America's black population. Later in 1963, as the planning of the March on Washington continued, 10,000 of these more radical blacks held their own meeting in the nation's capital. The convention took place at the Uline Arena, and its focus was on the Honorable Elijah Muhammad, a fragile-looking man with a slightly Oriental cast to his features, who held a Bible in one hand and a Koran, the Islamic book of revelations, in the other.

The 65-year-old Elijah Muhammad, dressed in a dark suit and bow tie, rose from his seat and walked to the podium. On his head, he wore a small, dark pillbox hat that was embroidered with images of a crescent moon, sun, and stars—symbols of the Islamic religion. Upon seeing their spiritual leader before them, the people in the crowd began to chant, "Little Lamb! Little Lamb!" which was the nickname they had given him. Then they cried out their greeting, "Praise be to Allah!"

Muhammad answered his disciples with what had become his familiar salutation: "*Asalaikum* [Peace be unto you] in the name of Allah, the most Merciful God, to whom all holy praises are due, the Lord of all the world, the most Merciful Father and life-giver to the lost-found mentally dead so called Negroes here in the Wilderness of North America."

Indeed, the man who was called the Messenger of Allah had been a central figure in the Lost-Found Nation of Islam in the Wilderness of North America

(now called the Muslim Community of America), whose followers are known as Black Muslims, for more than 30 years. Founded in the early 1930s by Wallace Fard, the Nation of Islam, with its message of black superiority and resistance to white domination, offered all of its supporters, particularly the black urban poor, a sense of mission in life. The theology of the Black Muslims claimed that all whites were devils who were about to fall from their positions of power. In their place would rise the black race, the chosen people of Allah.

The normally unassuming Muhammad usually described this scenario with the utmost intensity. Alex Haley and Alfred Balk, who attended one of the Black Muslim leader's speeches in early 1963, reported in

During the mid-20th century, Muhammad inspired tens of thousands of blacks to convert to the Lost-Found Nation of Islam. At the heart of the religious movement's message of black superiority was a profound faith in Allah, the supreme being of Islam.

Civil rights leader Martin Luther King, Jr. (front row, under flag), heads a 1965 demonstration to end racial discrimination in Montgomery, Alabama. A proponent of integration, King refused to employ violent means to achieve his goals. "Nonviolence," he maintained, "is the answer to the crucial political and moral questions of our time—the need for man to overcome oppression and violence without resorting to violence and oppression."

the *Saturday Evening Post*, "The tiny Muhammad sat impassively. Then, as he rose to speak, he seemed transformed. His movements became abrupt, jerky. He stared piercingly at his audience, spitting out his words in harsh, thin tones." And what magical words they proved to be.

By instilling racial self-esteem in the Black Muslims, Muhammad managed, in the words of author James Baldwin, "to heal and redeem drunkards and junkies, to convert people who have come out of prison and to keep them out, to make men chaste and women virtuous, and to invest both the male and the female with a pride and a serenity that hang about them like an unfailing light." In short, Muhammad accomplished what the church, the government, and other social institutions could not.

By the early 1960s, a time when black rights had emerged as the most burning issue in America, the

Nation of Islam had grown into a nation within a nation. Black Muslims, operating their own national newspaper and running their own businesses, claimed for themselves a significant amount of economic power. Yet the Nation's numerous temples and growing membership; its solid financial base; its problack theology; its fiery spokesman, Malcolm X; and its paramilitary branch, the Fruit of Islam, also made it a target for the fears of moderate blacks and most whites.

With the movement's message of black separatism adding its angry voice to the sounds of social unrest, the Nation of Islam, led by the paternal, delicate-looking Honorable Elijah Muhammad, stood as the most controversial of all movements at the height of the civil rights era. Muhammad was well prepared to deal with the controversy, however. He had known conflict all his life. •◊•

Nation of Islam minister Malcolm X addresses a New York rally in 1963. In calling for segregation and a violent revolution by blacks, he provided a marked contrast to the nonviolent protests of Martin Luther King, Jr., and other moderate civil rights leaders.

2

BLOCK

LIJAH MUHAMMAD WAS born under the name of Elijah Poole on October 7, 1897, at Bolds Springs, near Sandersville, Georgia, a small town between Macon and Atlanta. His first home was a sharecropper's shack that barely managed to accommodate Wali and Marie Poole's large family. Elijah was the sixth of their 13 children.

Right from the start, Elijah's mother sensed that he was special. As Elijah grew older, his brothers and sisters seemed to think so, too; they often asked him to settle their arguments because he was so levelheaded. In this respect, Elijah took after his father, a hardworking sharecropper who also served the local black population as a Baptist preacher.

In addition to giving instructive sermons in church every Sunday, Wali Poole was known to preach to his children. While Elijah was growing up, his father warned him not to stray from the long dirt road that led to the family's tenant farm near Sandersville. Under no circumstances, Wali Poole said, was Elijah to take a shortcut through the woods. Other children heading home from school might walk that way, but not he.

Elijah's curiosity was piqued, however, by that which was forbidden. Usually, his brothers or sisters

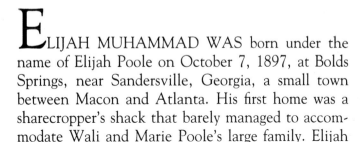

Destitute Georgia laborers use a primitive plow to till a field around the time of Elijah Muhammad's birth. For Muhammad, as for most black southerners, daily life at the turn of the century bore a great deal of similarity to life before slavery was abolished. "It is true that the law calls him a freeman," abolitionist and editor Frederick Douglass said of the black American, "but any white man, subjected to such restrictive and humiliating prohibitions, will certainly call himself a slave."

were with him when he left the family grounds. But one warm afternoon in the early 1900s, Elijah found himself alone on the dirt road. Everyone else was at the farm, preparing for the upcoming harvest. His parents had decided that a child such as Elijah would only get in the way. In the coming years, he would be expected to help out on the farm. But on this autumn day, his parents left him on his own.

As Elijah looked around the dirt road, the woods loomed large and inviting. At one point, he guessed that his family's small log cabin was on the other side of a clump of trees. Cutting a path through the woods would be the quickest way home, he realized. Elijah had never gone that way before, but he doubted that he would get lost. What he would do, he told himself,

THE UNITED STATES. |1900| B

.—POPULATION.   { Supervisor's District No. 1 0   Sheet No.
                 { Enumeration District No. 9 5   6

.... Name of Institution, ...

.... Thomas .... Spears ., Enumerator.   Ward of city, ...

A census of Clay County, Georgia, taken in 1900, lists Muhammad as Elija Pool (left column, 12th name from top). He was the sixth of 13 children.

was skirt the perimeter of the woods until he reached the edge of the field that his family farmed. Arriving there would put him just a stone's throw from his home.

As Elijah turned to enter the woods, he picked up a stick and threw it into the forest. He heard it clatter against a tree trunk before it fell on some ferns. A gentle breeze rustled the branches overhead.

As Elijah took a few steps underneath the green canopy, he felt a surge of guilt. He knew he was not supposed to venture any farther. Yet he balked at turning back. The mystery of the woods had a hold on him.

At first, Elijah walked slowly. He did not want to arrive home too early, or else his mother might realize that he had taken a shortcut. He picked up a stick and ran around the trees, enjoying his little adventure. Then he stretched out on the grass. There was no reason to avoid the woods, he reasoned. It was a fun place. From now on, he would go there whenever he felt like it.

Elijah was still lying on the ground, watching the patterns of the branches against the sky, when he heard the dull thump of approaching boots. Then came the muffled sound of voices. Perhaps, Elijah thought, he had spent too much time in the woods, prompting his mother to send a few of his brothers to look for him. If they found him, he would certainly be punished.

With his heart beating quickly, the young boy scampered into a nearby thicket and peered through the brambles. When he saw that the approaching figures were not his brothers, he felt relieved. Then, as the people came closer, his sense of relief turned to a mixture of fear and disbelief.

There were four people. At the head of the small party was a white man holding on to a rope. At the

Sandersville, Georgia, where Muhammad spent his early years. Like most black children in the rural South, he attended school only when he was not needed on the farm. "My going to school no further than the fourth grade," he said later of his limited education, "proves that I can know nothing except the truth I have been taught by Allah."

other end of the rope was a black man, who had it tied about his midsection, as though he were a horse or a mule. They were followed by two more white men in work clothes. These two pushed the captured black, whose hands were tied behind his back, to keep him moving. Was this some kind of game? Elijah wondered.

Suddenly, the hidden boy recognized the black man—Elijah had seen him in town. He sometimes attended the church where Elijah's father preached. The man looked frightened now, although he was trying hard not to let the others detect how afraid he was. Even when he tripped and fell heavily, his eyes remained fixed in a faraway stare.

Elijah wanted to shout out to the fallen man, but he felt as though his own body were frozen with fear. When the whites began kicking their prisoner and insulting him, Elijah buckled as if he, too, had been kicked. Silent tears rolled down his face.

The man in front proceeded to untie the rope around the black man's wrists. He took one end of the rope and threw it over a sturdy branch. Leering at his captive, who still lay facedown on the forest floor, he formed the other end into a noose. Then he slipped the hooped rope around the black man's neck. Elijah covered his face with his hands as the victim was hoisted from the ground, spluttering and choking.

It only took a matter of minutes. After the lynchers were sure the man was dead, they passed a bottle among themselves and looked up at his body, admiring their handiwork. Then, as though they had just concluded an entire day's work, they strolled away, leaving the strangled black man swinging from the tree.

The woods were silent except for the sniffles of a small boy. Elijah wiped his eyes and crawled from his hiding place. He wanted to run away as fast as he could, to get away from the lifeless face and the hang-man's noose. But something prevented him from doing so.

As if in a trance, Elijah made his way to where a worn shoe had fallen to the ground. The shoe looked as though it had simply been mislaid and whoever had lost it would return to claim it. Elijah crouched down to touch the shoe.

Suddenly, something wet and warm dripped onto the back of his neck. Elijah attempted to brush away whatever it was; he was still transfixed by the shoe. Then he noticed that his fingertips were covered by a rich red color. Elijah looked up and saw that blood was trickling down the dead man's foot.

This gruesome scene would continue to haunt Elijah for many years. Instead of fading from his mem-ory, the nightmarish incident would serve as a vivid reminder to him of the brutal treatment that blacks, especially those in the South, were known to suffer. From 1882 to 1968, nearly 3,500 blacks (3 times the number of whites) were lynched in the United States. Many more were terrorized by whites but were spared the hangman's noose.

To be a southern black at the turn of the century usually meant a life of hardship and pain as well as danger. By the turn of the century, a wide variety of segregation laws—popularly known as Jim Crow laws—had been established to take away many of the constitutional rights that had been granted to blacks in the years immediately following the Civil War. These segregation laws, which called for separate but equal public facilities for blacks and whites, invariably led to separate but *unequal* accommodations for blacks.

Moreover, a number of high-handed methods kept blacks from exercising their recently won right to vote. Ballot-box stuffing; "white" primaries, which excluded blacks from participating in the preelection

A horrible testament to the racial hatred that permeated the South in which Muhammad was raised: a black lynch victim hanged by whites. Having witnessed a similar scene in his youth, Muhammad often drew on the incident during talks with his followers.

Muhammad spent much of his early twenties scouring Georgia for a way to earn a better living than sharecropping, his family's principal occupation. In 1922, he signed on as a laborer at the Cherokee Brick and Tile Company (right and opposite) in Macon.

process; and complicated registration and voting procedures that kept blacks away from the voting booth were some of the ways by which they were denied their right to political representation. By 1908, eight states—Alabama, Louisiana, Mississippi, North Carolina, Oklahoma, South Carolina, Virginia, and Georgia—had revised their constitutions to disfranchise most blacks.

While Elijah was growing up, he was acutely aware of the problems that besieged blacks in the United States. His family, like most sharecroppers, barely managed to make ends meet. In the early 1900s, tenant farming was a common practice in the South. Sharecroppers rented the land they farmed from a local landowner in return for a portion of the season's crop. They sold the remaining portion for a small sum of money—just enough to buy a few articles of clothing and some basic supplies.

To help pay their debts, sharecroppers were often compelled to borrow from white creditors, who, spotting an easy mark, lent money to the farmers at exorbitant interest rates. The Pooles fell victim to this vicious cycle. Added to their hardship of laboring long hours for next to nothing was the ever-increasing amount of money they owed their white creditors.

When Elijah was 6 years old, Wali Poole decided to move his family nearly 100 miles southwest, to Weona, Georgia, a small town located 5 miles from Cordele. The Pooles rented a house across the street from the railroad depot, where a train stopped once each day. In Weona, Wali Poole again attempted to scratch out a living as a sharecropper.

Elijah, like all of the Poole children, attended school except when their father asked them to work the fields. Despite having a delicate constitution, Elijah prided himself on contributing as much as his

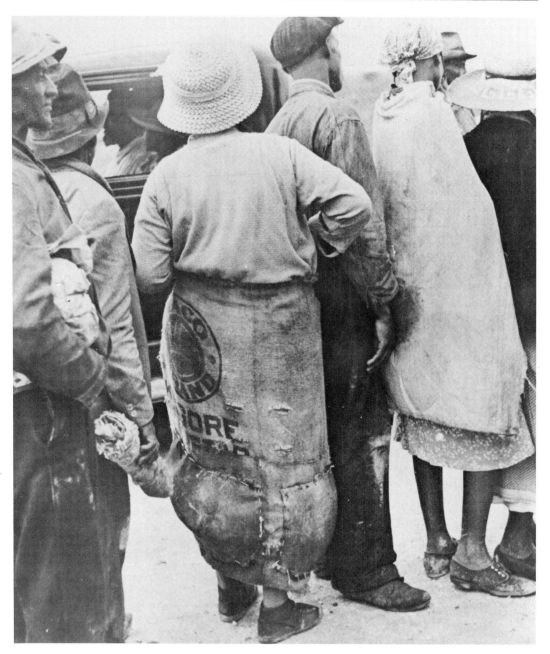

In 1923, Muhammad and his family joined the millions of blacks who migrated to the North in search of better jobs and living conditions. Life in Detroit, Michigan, where Muhammad settled, and other northern cities proved to be more accommodating, until the Great Depression struck in 1929.

brothers and sisters to the family's welfare. He plowed behind a mule, sowed the fields in the spring, and reaped the crops at harvesttime. After completing the fifth grade at the age of 14, he left school to work full-time as a hired field hand and sawmill worker.

Although Elijah no longer attended classes, he continued to educate himself. Upon returning home after laboring from dawn to dusk, he had one of his older sisters tutor him. Years later, Elijah's mother remembered him pouring over the Scriptures with tears in his eyes. Elijah said that he cried out of frustrated desire; he badly wanted to experience the salvation that the Bible promised. Listening to his father's fiery Sunday sermons also made Elijah long to be released from the oppression he saw all around him.

During his teens, Elijah exhibited the same quiet authority that had earned him the respect of his older brothers and sisters when he was a child. Disapproving of the verbal abuse that his white employers frequently leveled at black workers, he would speak to his employers in a calm and reasonable voice. "I would ask them to just fire me if they didn't like my work," he recalled, "but don't curse me." Because of his polite manner and honest reputation, he was often put in charge of the other black workers.

Elijah left home when he was 16 but continued to live and work in the same area. Two years later, in 1915, he met Clara Evans in a church meetinghouse. She had been born in nearby Houston County, where her father maintained an unusual degree of independence by renting his land for money instead of sharecropping it.

One of Clara's sisters, Rose, remembered Elijah's visits to the Evans home on Sunday afternoons after church. He was a polite, reserved young man, who tended to wear a blue suit and tie. He would arrive punctually at six o'clock in the evening and leave by nine because he had to get up early to work in the fields the next day.

After two years of courtship, Clara Evans and Elijah Poole eloped. They were married on May 2, 1917. After a monthlong honeymoon, the newlyweds returned to Weona and moved in with Elijah's brother Sam and his family. The two families lived together in a dilapidated wooden shack that belonged to a white landowner named Thompson, who also owned the land the Poole brothers sharecropped.

Clara and Elijah Poole's first son, Emmanuel, was born on February 3, 1921, in Clara's parents' home. With a growing family to feed—all told, he would have 19 children—Elijah Poole looked for a more lucrative way to earn a living. He could not find any work locally, so he left his wife and newborn son at home and began to search for employment in another area. Emmanuel was one and a half years old when his father finally sent for the family to join him. He had found work in Macon as an employee for the Cherokee Brick and Tile Company.

Shortly thereafter, Poole began working for the Southern Railroad Company, where Jim Crow laws were strictly enforced. A white railway worker described his feelings toward his black co-workers in the following manner: "In the railway mail service there are a great many Negroes. . . . It is unpleasant for whites to work with [them], where it is almost impossible to have different drinking vessels and different towels or places to wash." Another white railway worker voiced a similar attitude: "We are assured that Negroes cannot object to segregation—it is the best thing for them as well as ourselves."

Racial segregation applied to railroad passengers as well as workers. In 1891, Georgia had passed a law that made it illegal for a black to sit in the same car as a white. By 1900, all southern states had enacted similar laws—in waiting rooms, rest rooms, railroad cars, and streetcars. As always, these Jim Crow laws resulted in inferior facilities for blacks.

The attitude of the white South toward its black inhabitants often led to moments of extreme racial tension. As blacks were reduced to the status of second-class citizens, southern whites intimidated blacks to keep them "in their place." It has been estimated that in the first decade of the 20th century, 40 major race riots took place, with the worst rioting occurring in 1906 in Atlanta, about 100 miles from where Elijah Poole lived. According to official figures, 10 blacks were killed in the Atlanta riot and 60 more were badly beaten.

In 1923, the one thing that Poole dreaded most came to pass: One of his white employers physically accosted him. Poole decided to avoid further trouble by moving his family north, to Detroit, Michigan. Looking back at his life in Georgia, he commented: "I saw enough of the white man's brutality to last me 26,000 years."

3

"FRIENDS OF THE RACE"

❧

IN LEAVING THE South, the Pooles became part of a vast black migration. During the first 3 decades of the 20th century, approximately 3 million blacks left the South to seek their fortunes in the promised land of the North. According to a 1910 census, nine-tenths of the nation's black population lived in the South, with three out of four blacks residing in rural areas. Fifty years later, three-quarters of all black Americans lived in northern cities.

Although blacks had been moving north since the time of the Civil War, the largest migration boom occurred around World War I, when nearly a half million rural blacks left the South. Race relations certainly played a part in this mass exodus. But the primary force behind the shift in population was an economic one.

In the early 1910s, cotton plantations in the South were devastated by a sudden influx of beetles called boll weevils. These cotton-eating insects entered the United States through Mexico and gradually ate their way eastward, ravaging cotton crops throughout the South and drastically reducing the already limited holdings of black tenant farmers. Moreover, hundreds of thousands of blacks were left homeless in 1915, when flood waters washed over riverbanks in Alabama and Mississippi.

During this same period, World War I stimulated economic growth in the industrial North. Factories that manufactured military equipment had to increase their productivity, and unskilled and semiskilled la-

A hooded member of the Ku Klux Klan, a white supremacist organization, dangles a hangman's noose as a grim reminder to blacks to keep their distance from white society. In response to such warnings, blacks often banded together to form their own organizations and movements.

borers found themselves in great demand to help speed up production. Northern manufacturers went so far as to send industrial agents into the South to search for men to fill the positions left vacant by those who had gone to war. So acute was the shortage of workers that these agents sometimes paid transportation costs for entire families to move north.

Filled with the hope of finding more work opportunities and a better life in northern urban centers, most of these black migrants referred to the North as "the Promised Land." Yet for the majority of blacks, life in northern cities proved to be anything but ideal. As World War I came to an end, the urgent call for more manpower ceased. Jobs became harder to find because the armistice caused a sudden decrease in manufacturing needs. Moreover, the men who had fought in the war were ready to rejoin the work force. As the competition for jobs grew fierce, the over-abundance of men scrambling for a limited number of positions led to racial friction. Not surprisingly, job-seeking whites felt threatened by the large number of blacks also looking for work.

In 1917, one year before the war ended, the animosity of white workers erupted into race riots in both Philadelphia and Chester, Pennsylvania. In July of that same year, the black ghetto of East St. Louis, Illinois, witnessed one of the worst race riots of the century. The violent outburst began when a group of whites in a Ford rode through East St. Louis, randomly spraying gunfire into black homes. As night fell, some blacks mistook a police car for the Ford driven by the white joyriders and shot at the car. Two policemen were killed.

Later that night, the whites retaliated. They burned down the homes of blacks and killed the occupants as they attempted to flee from the burning buildings. At least 39 people were hanged, clubbed, shot, or stabbed to death. A few weeks later, a similar series of hostile events precipitated a riot in Houston, Texas.

By 1919, racial relations in America were steadily deteriorating. Activist and editor W. E. B. Du Bois urged blacks in the May issue of the *Crisis*, the widely read journal published by the National Association for the Advancement of Colored People (NAACP), the nation's leading antidiscrimination organization, to respond to this postwar shift in fortunes with militant action: "We return from the slavery of the uniform which the world's madness demanded us to don to the freedom of civil garb. . . . *We return. We return from fighting. We return fighting.* Make way for Democracy!" But white America had other ideas. Later that year, race riots broke out in about two dozen cities across the United States, including Washington, D.C., Knoxville, Tennessee, and Chicago, Illinois. All told, more than 60 blacks were lynched, yielding a steady stream of bloodshed that prompted James Weldon Johnson, NAACP field secretary, to refer to the season with the greatest number of riots as "the Red Summer."

Racial tensions were still running high four years later, when Elijah Poole traveled north to Detroit with his wife, Clara, and their young son, Emmanuel, and settled in a house that lacked many bare essentials, including a toilet. During the 1920s, the house would hold three more Poole children: Ethel, Nathaniel, and Lotte. Clara would help support the family by working as a domestic.

Poole's first job in Detroit was at the American Can Factory. After that, he took a spot on the assembly line at the Chevrolet Motor Company, where the work was as backbreaking as it was tedious. His soft-spoken manner made him popular with his fellow workers, and his dependability impressed his white employers. But because he was black, there was little opportunity for economic advancement.

One of the most influential black activists in the first half of the 20th century, W. E. B. Du Bois called on the educated black elite to pressure whites into allowing the full benefits of American society to blacks. "This is our country," he wrote at the end of World War I. "We have worked for it, we have suffered for it, we have fought for it."

Armed federal troops in Chicago watch over black civilians after a race riot during the "Red Summer" of 1919. When Muhammad moved to the North four years later, racial relations remained extremely tense.

One of the ways that blacks responded to their lowly plight was by organizing themselves. And in the early 1920s, no black was playing a greater role in bringing his people together than Marcus Garvey. An advocate of racial separatism, he promoted a unique vision that captured the imagination of blacks across the nation.

As a young man, Garvey campaigned, both in his native Jamaica and in Central America, against the brutal treatment of his fellow West Indian workers. These efforts met with little success, but rather than give up, he traveled to London in 1912 with the hope of persuading the British government to change its policies toward colonial workers. Once again, Garvey was unable to find a way to alleviate the suffering of the workers. But the trip paid dividends nonetheless. While in Europe, he traveled and read extensively. The most influential book Garvey studied was Booker T. Washington's autobiography, *Up from Slavery*, an inspiring account of how the educator rose from being a janitor to the status of America's leading black spokesman.

Upon returning to Jamaica in 1914, Garvey founded the Universal Negro Improvement Association (UNIA), an organization intent on promoting black pride. When the UNIA failed to take hold in Jamaica, Garvey shifted its headquarters in 1916 to Harlem, New York's black district. By 1919, the UNIA had found its supporters; the organization claimed a worldwide membership of 2 million.

At the heart of Garvey's movement was his desire to see blacks educate themselves so that they could achieve economic independence and political power. He urged blacks to shed their sense of disillusionment, to take pride in their race, and to dream of a brighter future. Garvey fostered this program by proving himself to be an emotional speaker as well as a consummate actor. "Where is the black man's Government?"

he would ask. "Where is his King, and his kingdom, his navy, his men of big affairs?" Telling his listeners that he had never seen such things, he would declare: "I will help to make them."

And so he did. The UNIA thrilled blacks everywhere by staging spectacular parades in Harlem, especially the one held in August 1920 during the International Convention of the Negro Peoples of the World. The UNIA delegates, who came to New York from as far away as Africa and South America, met throughout the month in the organization's headquarters at Liberty Hall. The convention featured religious services and a silent march through Harlem in addition to conferences and speeches.

But it was the magnificent parade that the UNIA organized through the Harlem streets that garnered the most attention and encouraged people to join Garvey's ranks. The parade was led by members of the African legions, wearing blue military uniforms with bright red stripes on their trousers. Riding on horseback, these marchers possessed a military bearing that suggested the hidden power of the black race.

Following these riders were 200 Black Cross nurses in long white dresses and white stockings. Although few of these women were actually nurses, they symbolized the UNIA's commitment to aiding the sick and needy members of the black community. The rest of the parade included the Juveniles, a group of proud young Garveyites; thousands of delegates who had come at Garvey's request to discuss the current condition of black life; and a choir.

Garvey himself rode in an open car, like a head of state. He wore a uniform with fringed epaulets and carried a cane in white-gloved hands. Although he was short in stature, his long-plumed helmet made him easy to single out as the leader of the parade.

Garvey was easy to single out in another way: Unlike the nation's more moderate black leaders,

such as W. E. B. Du Bois, and less radical movements, such as the NAACP, he strongly opposed
integration efforts. In fact, as the 1920s progressed,
Garvey promoted himself as a Black Moses striving
to lead his people back to their African homeland.
Though this heady dream never came to fruition,
black separatist groups kept his Back to Africa con-
cept alive for many decades to come.

Garvey did not look only to promote a euphoric
sense of hope among his followers. His organization
produced some concrete results. He published a black
newspaper, *Negro World*, and encouraged the formation of numerous black businesses. He even began
his own shipping company, the Black Star Line, an
economic venture operated solely by blacks. The
shipping company's aim was to link black commerce
all over the world and to transport black Americans
to their African homeland.

Despite its initial success, the UNIA soon fal-
tered. In 1922, Garvey surprised many of his follow-

*Thousands of spectators line a
street in the Harlem district of
New York to watch a parade held
in 1920 by the Universal Negro
Improvement Association
(UNIA), a black nationalist organization founded by Marcus
Garvey. Muhammad became a
member of Garvey's movement in
the mid-1920s.*

ers. In an attempt to gain support for his Back to Africa movement, he formed a pact with the Ku Klux Klan (KKK), a white supremacist organization that was notorious for its violent attacks against blacks. Although he never claimed any abiding love for the Klan, Garvey believed that he and the KKK stood on similar ground on one important issue: The Klan wanted blacks out of the country, and Garvey desired them out, too. Because they both wholeheartedly supported racial separatism, Garvey went so far as to say that Klansmen were "better friends of the [black] race" than the NAACP.

In forming such a strange alliance with the Klan, Garvey spurred moderate blacks, especially those in the black press, to attack the UNIA. He supplied them with even more ammunition to carry out their campaign when the Black Star Line, whose finances he had seriously mismanaged from the start, fell into utter ruin. Matters grew worse for Garvey in 1923, when he was convicted of mail fraud—he had made illegal use of America's postal service by selling phony stock for his shipping enterprise.

As the Black Star Line sank, the UNIA went down with it. Garvey was sent to a federal penitentiary in Atlanta, Georgia, in 1925, and two years later, after serving half of his five-year prison sentence, he was deported to Jamaica. U.S. officials never again allowed him entry into America.

While Garvey had been launching the UNIA, another black nationalist movement was being formed: Noble Drew Ali's Moorish Temple of America. Ali fired the imagination of lower-class blacks and amassed a large following by claiming that blacks were superior to whites. The white race, he added, was doomed.

According to Ali's followers, the Moorish Temple of America was founded after the North Carolina–born Ali visited Morocco. There the king told Ali

The rise of Marcus Garvey: A master at theatrics, black nationalist leader Garvey was dressed in full uniform as he took part in the UNIA's August 1920 parade through Harlem.

to teach Islam to black Americans. Ali established his first temple in Newark, New Jersey, in 1915 and urged all black Americans to refer to themselves as Moorish Americans.

As his teachings spread to the Midwest, Ali issued national identification cards to his followers. These cards bore the symbols of Islam: a star and crescent, an image of clasped hands, and an encircled number seven. The cards also declared that the bearer believed in "all the Divine Prophets, Jesus, Muhammad, Buddha and Confucius."

The fall of Marcus Garvey: Federal marshals escort a handcuffed Garvey from a New York train station in 1925, after the appeal of his conviction for mail fraud was rejected.

Ali's version of Islam was derived from a variety of sources: Eastern philosophy, the Koran, and the Bible. It also drew on assorted anecdotes from Jesus Christ and, as the UNIA leader gained more and more attention, Marcus Garvey. Followers of the Moorish Temple of America were forbidden to go to movies and dance halls and were not supposed to use cosmetics, hair straighteners, tobacco, or alcohol. Ali's teachings put an emphasis on a healthy diet and natural herbal remedies. A sample recipe was billed as Old Moorish Herb Tea for Human Ailments.

To make themselves appear more like their African counterparts, Ali's male followers each donned a red fez and grew a beard. Accompanying this new look was an open contempt for police as well as whites, whom the Moorish Americans called Europeans. Ali's teachings were paired with the selling of charms, relics, magical potions, and pictures that were associated with blacks of supposedly Islamic origin.

By the mid-1920s, Ali's movement had attracted droves of newcomers, many of whom had previously been Garveyites. In 1929, however, he was implicated in the murder of the philanthropist Julius Rosenwald, and his movement fell apart. Shortly thereafter, Ali died from what were said to be mysterious causes.

The notion of black separatist organizations struck a deep chord in Elijah Poole, who joined Garvey's movement shortly after arriving in Detroit and quickly rose to the position of corporal in the Chicago division of the UNIA. As an ardent Garveyite, he became greatly discouraged by the demise of the movement. But by the end of the 1920s, he was fretting over more than the decline and fall of Marcus Garvey.

Barely managing to make ends meet throughout the decade, Poole saw the crash of the New York Stock Exchange in 1929 ravage the entire nation. This collapse heralded the beginning of an economic depression that lasted well into World War II. Millions of unskilled laborers lost their jobs during these years of financial crisis, and black workers were usually the first to be let go by their employers. Before the crash, the average wage for blacks in Detroit was 55 cents an hour. During the 1930s, this amount dropped to 10 cents—for those fortunate enough to be employed at all in the depression years.

Soup kitchens were set up to offer free meals to the unemployed. At the Detroit branch of the state's department of welfare, which disbursed federal relief funds to the public, lines of needy people seeking aid snaked out the building and around the block. As the end of the decade approached, two out of every three families in Detroit were applying for subsistence welfare.

Poole was among those who lost their jobs in 1929 and stood on relief lines. He and his family faced extremely lean times. The Pooles often subsisted on such meals as chicken feet and vegetable leaves. Coal for the kitchen stove, which was used to heat the house, was collected from the beds along the railroad tracks. Nothing of even the slightest use was thrown away. The four Poole children wore hand-me-downs given to Clara by the people for whom she cleaned, washed, and ironed. The youngsters never seemed to know the original color of these clothes, for most of the material was covered with patches. And the hard-

Father Divine (center), founder of the Father Divine Peace Mission, a religious movement that aided poor blacks, hurls pieces of paper with prayers written on them into the air. Like Muhammad, he was the son of Georgia sharecroppers and went on to establish branches of his movement nationwide.

ship did not stop there. The soles of their shoes had to be reinforced with cardboard. Sometimes Emmanuel borrowed his mother's shoes and wore them to school, kicking them off as he drew near the building so his classmates would not see them and laugh at him.

Poole remained on relief until 1931. He had no other alternative. Every morning, he left home before dawn to join the lines of thousands of unemployed people that formed in front of the gates of the local manufacturing plants. He often waited there all morning, hoping to be hired for a day's work, only to return home empty-handed to his hungry children.

As living conditions grew progressively worse, blacks turned to new or budding organizations and religious movements for leadership and spiritual guidance. For those interested in forming a black homeland overseas, there was the Peace Movement of Ethiopia, which supported the racist Mississippi senator Theodore G. Bilbo's bill to repatriate black Americans to Africa. The National Movement for the Establishment of the 49th State sought to create a black state within the United States. The Father Divine Peace Missions emerged as another popular movement. Led by George Baker, who had assumed the name Father Divine in the early 1900s, the peace missions won legions of followers by providing low-cost or free food to poor blacks during the depression.

Among the more radical movements was the Lost-Found Nation of Islam. During the summer of 1930, a small, earnest brown-skinned man who usually went by the name of Wallace Fard arrived in Detroit. Acting as a door-to-door peddler, he quickly managed to make himself welcome in the homes of the misnamed Paradise Valley, the city's black neighborhood. Fard told his prospective customers that the silk items he was selling had been worn by blacks in their ancestral homeland across the Atlantic.

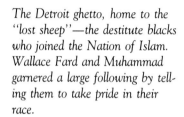

The Detroit ghetto, home to the "lost sheep"—the destitute blacks who joined the Nation of Islam. Wallace Fard and Muhammad garnered a large following by telling them to take pride in their race.

A short time later, after he had gained their confidence, Fard began to hold meetings that were devoted to a topic other than business. Fard claimed to be a prophet from Arabia who had come to the United States to help black Americans discover their dual African and Islamic heritage. He told his listeners that they, not whites, were the chosen people. The first humans to walk the earth had been black, he said, "long before the white man stood up on his hind legs and crept out of the caves of Europe."

The white man, Fard continued, was the devil himself. The embodiment of evil, whites had enslaved the blacks and had robbed them of their African names, giving them Christian names instead. To reclaim their rightful place in the world, blacks should adopt an Islamic name or use an X or combination of X's and other letters to symbolize a spiritual rebirth. With Fard's help, and that of the Nation of Islam, blacks would learn to respect their heritage, gain a sense of discipline, and work to overcome their white oppressors.

Fard's teachings varied significantly from those of traditional Islam, which promotes brotherhood between people of all races. His religious movement, in fact, had much more in common with Garvey's black nationalism and Ali's Moorish Temple of America. As a result, he attracted to the Nation of Islam many of the same people who had been drawn to Garvey and Ali. Fard's "lost sheep" subsequently became known as Black Muslims.

Among those who attended Fard's evening seminars, which were usually held in a Detroit tenement basement, was Elijah Poole. He later said of Fard, "I recognized him to be God in person and that is what he said he was, but he forbade me to tell anyone else. I was a student of the Bible. I recognized him to be the person the Bible predicted would come two thousand years after Jesus' death. It came to me the first time I laid eyes on him."

Certain that Fard was a holy man, Poole became one of his first converts and was given an Islamic name. From that day on, he was known as Elijah Muhammad. ✿

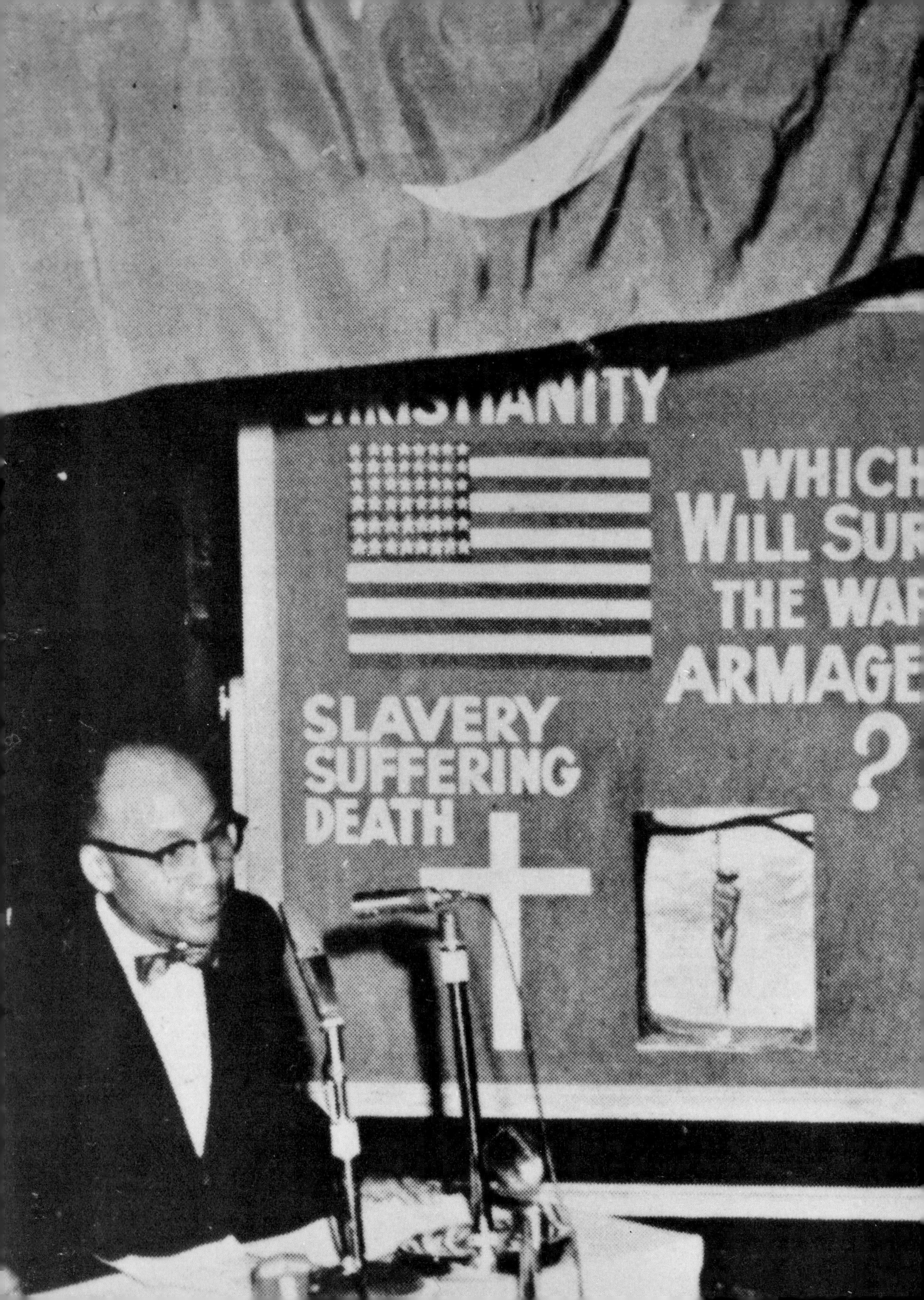
WHICH
WILL SUR
THE WAR
ARMAGE
?
SLAVERY
SUFFERING
DEATH

4

TRIBULATIONS

WHEN ELIJAH POOLE joined the Nation of Islam in 1931 and took the name Elijah Muhammad, two of his brothers and his wife converted as well. From then on, Clara Poole was known as Sister Clara—"Sister" being the proper title for addressing a Black Muslim woman. She also adopted the modest style of dress prescribed by Wallace Fard, which involved covering her head with a white headdress and wearing a floor-length white garment.

Muhammad became Fard's chief lieutenant and helped him rouse support for the Nation of Islam during the early 1930s by offering a message of hope to blacks. Chief among their tasks was the establishment of Islamic temples, or mosques, in converted stores in a number of midwestern cities. By 1934, Fard, with Muhammad's help, had recruited 8,000 people to his movement. Many of these converts were poor blacks from the urban ghettos. Like Muhammad, they had migrated from the rural South and were gravely disappointed by life in the North.

As the Nation grew in size, Fard chose to remain a man of unusual mystery. He went by several names, including Wali Farrad, Professor Ford, Farrad Mohammed, F. Mohammed Ali, and, on occasion, Allah. He supposedly told one of his earliest converts,

Muhammad uses a bulletin board to illustrate his teachings during a meeting in a Nation of Islam temple. He often asked his followers to compare what he claimed were the tenets of Christianity— "slavery, suffering, death"—to those of Islam—"freedom, justice, equality"—and then to ascertain which group Allah had chosen to let survive after the destruction of the world.

"My name is W. D. Fard, and I come from the Holy City of Mecca. More about myself I will not tell you yet, for the time has not yet come. I am your brother. You have not yet seen me in my royal robes."

Fard, whose name in Arabic means the first part of an early-morning Islamic prayer, let some details slip about his past. He said that he was born in Africa as a member of the Kuraish tribe—the same tribe as the founder of Islam, the Prophet Muhammad, who lived from around 570 to 632. Fard also claimed that he was educated in England and later at the Uni-

Black Muslim women study Arabic in a Nation of Islam school. Although the movement's precepts differed significantly from fundamental Islam, many of the Nation's practices—including diet, prayer, and dress—were similar to Islamic teachings.

versity of Southern California and had been trained for a diplomatic career.

Though Fard may have embellished or exaggerated the details of his life, the origins of his teachings were not quite so mysterious. The Nation drew its principles not only from the Koran but also from the Bible, books about Freemasonry, and the philosophy of Joseph F. ("Judge") Rutherford, leader of the Jehovah's Witnesses. Fard's movement also borrowed from such titles as Story of Mankind and The Conquest of Civilization.

Fard himself wrote esoteric manuals defining his religious movement: *The Secret Ritual for the Nation of Islam* (whose contents are now passed on orally by Black Muslims) and *Teaching for the Lost-Found Nation of Islam in a Mathematical Way*. The latter publication, which Fard had filled with symbolic language, was handed out to newly enlisted Black Muslims.

The Nation's story of creation had a unique twist, making it markedly different from those of other religious groups. According to Fard, the world was initially ruled by members of a black race who were known as the original men. Theirs was a highly advanced civilization, and their scientists formed mountains and seas, covered the land with animals, and blasted the moon, which had been part of the earth, into the sky. Some of the original men settled in Arabia and became known as the Tribe of Shabazz. They lived in peace, worshiping Allah from the holy city of Mecca, until evil entered the world in the form of a mad scientist named Yacub. Full of pride, Yacub broke the laws of Islam and was exiled from Mecca. His heart set on vengeance, he applied his knowledge of genetics to create a race of immoral men, the white devils.

The whites caused endless trouble for the blacks until they were herded together and exiled to the cold wasteland of Europe. Allah then sent his black prophets Moses and Jesus to convert the white devils to Islam. Instead, the whites distorted the prophets' teachings and founded the blasphemous religions of Judaism and Christianity.

Fulfilling an ancient prophecy, the whites gained dominion over the entire world. They transported millions of blacks from Africa to the Americas in slave ships and stripped them of their language and cultural heritage. Along the way, blacks were brainwashed into thinking that whites were their superiors.

Fard claimed it was time for the reign of the whites to end.

The leader of the Nation taught that there was neither a heaven nor a hell after death. Both heaven and hell existed here on earth, and blacks had been living in hell for nearly 400 years. Whites, or, as Fard sometimes called them, "blue-eyed devils," had created the black man's hell.

In the Islamic tradition, the savior, who will one day redeem all men lost in an earthly hell, is called the Mahdi. This mighty being is both a person and God. Fard told the Black Muslims that the Mahdi was none other than himself and that he was going to lead blacks to the state of grace from which they had fallen so long ago. As the Mahdi, he was the instrument of redemption. Under his leadership, the Nation of Islam would establish a utopian paradise, a separate territory within the United States that would be ruled only by blacks.

Wallace Fard, the founder of the Nation of Islam, as photographed on May 26, 1933, by the Detroit police department, which referred to the Black Muslims as a diabolic "voodoo cult" and had Fard and his followers under constant surveillance. Fard subsequently moved the center of the Nation's operations to Chicago.

Muhammad and his son Wallace pose beneath a portrait of Wallace Fard. According to the Nation of Islam's teachings, Fard, who claimed he was Allah, passed on the mantle of the Nation's leadership to Allah's messenger, Muhammad.

Fard's critics denounced his religious doctrines and his proclamation of divine authority. Yet his supporters, the downtrodden race of American society, believed in him and his message of racial pride. To the Black Muslims, the history of mankind according to Fard was no less believable than the story of creation that is told in the Bible.

Among the reasons why Fard garnered so many followers was that he gave direction to their lives. He required them to adhere to a special diet and to refrain from the use of alcohol, drugs, and cigarettes. Aspire to personal discipline, thriftiness, and cleanliness, he told them.

The Nation offered its support to help Fard's disciples meet these goals. A temple was established in Detroit, and programs were set up to educate Black Muslims and to help them form their own restaurants, markets, and other businesses within the black community. The University of Islam, a combined elementary and secondary school for Black Muslim children and their parents, was founded in Detroit as well. Fard also established the Muslim Girls' Training Class, which taught young women the principles of home economics and proper social behavior. And he organized the Fruit of Islam, a tightly knit corps of adult males who were instructed in religious doctrine and the art of self-defense.

Despite these achievements, Fard, like Marcus Garvey and Noble Drew Ali before him, attracted the attention of the police. The air of mystery surrounding the Black Muslims' closely knit society led to rumors that the Nation was a cult that practiced human sacrifice. In the spring of 1933, the Detroit police ordered Fard to leave town. He sought refuge in Chicago, where Elijah Muhammad had established the Nation's Temple Number Two the previous year.

Immediately upon reaching Chicago, Fard was arrested by the authorities. Behind prison bars, he sent for Muhammad, whose devotion to the Black Muslim leader had resulted in a deep friendship, and appointed him chief minister. Muhammad stepped in as head of Temple Number One in Detroit and took charge of the movement's administrative functions.

It was not an easy task. Just as Muhammad assumed the leadership of the Nation, tensions between the Black Muslims and the police in Detroit were reaching a climax. The Michigan State Board of Education had notified the Detroit authorities that the Nation was running an unaccredited school. The police responded by arresting the teachers at the University of Islam.

These arrests were tied to the case of Sally Allah, a young Black Muslim who had left public school to attend the University of Islam. Black Muslims were allegedly surrounding the public schools and telling black children to leave them and study instead at the University of Islam. There they would be taught black history by blacks and learn Arabic, the language of the Koran.

Upon hearing of the arrests, Muhammad went to the jail where the university teachers were housed and offered himself up for arrest. The police charged him with contributing to the delinquency of a minor. When a local radio station announced that Muhammad was in official custody, 700 unarmed Black Muslims marched to police headquarters to stage a protest. They were greeted, however, by a number of billy club–wielding police who forced the crowd to disperse.

The authorities eventually dropped the charges against Muhammad and the university, provided that the Black Muslims enroll their children in the public school system within the next six months. Muhammad refused to comply with this order. Instead, he moved his ever-growing family to Chicago.

Shortly after this episode, around June 1934, Fard disappeared from the public—as mysteriously, it seems, as he had arrived. Many of his people said that he had returned to Mecca to ready himself for the end of the world. Others said that he had met with foul play at the hands of the police. Although Muhammad claimed that Fard had been deported, critics of the Black Muslim movement observed that Fard's disappearance and Muhammad's subsequent rise to power were not coincidental.

In any event, infighting broke out within the Nation following Fard's disappearance, and membership dwindled. At odds with some of the movement's factions, Muhammad established a separate branch of the Nation: the Temple People, who were members of a sect called the Allah Temple of Islam.

During the early days of this faction, attendance at the meetings was low. Yet under Muhammad's leadership, the Allah Temple of Islam eventually surpassed in size the original Nation of Islam. As Muhammad's movement grew, its meetings were shifted from private homes in Chicago to rented halls in the city's South Side ghetto. These meeting places became known as the Temples of Islam.

In time, Fard's entire network was replaced, but he was not forgotten. The Black Muslims, now led by Muhammad, deified Fard and proclaimed his birthday, February 26, as Savior's Day. Elijah Muhammad, whom Fard had designated to lead the Nation's faithful to the kingdom of God, became known as the Messenger of Allah. 〰

5

"FREEDOM OR DEATH?"

❦

T HE BLACK MUSLIM movement captured the public's attention once again on March 5, 1935. A family of Black Muslims was taken to court in Chicago because of a conflict on a city bus, and they brought along about 50 supporters from the movement. As the day wore on, all charges against the family were dropped. But when the Nation of Islam followers tried to leave the courtroom, they mistakenly tried to exit at the rear. The bailiffs informed them that the proper exit was at the front of the room, and in the confusion several Black Muslim women were pushed. A few of the men responded by seizing chairs and swinging them at the court authorities.

"Aroused to an almost fanatical frenzy by the chain of small incidents that ordinarily would have passed unnoticed in the crowded courtroom," the *Chicago Tribune* reported, "the cultists, their red crescent-marked fezzes askew, stormed through the room." It took a half hour and 150 policemen and bailiffs to quell the brawl. Forty-three Black Muslims were arrested. Forty of them were jailed two days later on the charge of contempt of court.

Black Muslims in Chicago were in conflict not only with the police. Continued internal fighting for

A handcuffed Muhammad is led to jail by a federal marshal, who arrested the Nation of Islam leader in 1942 for draft evasion. "The devils do not respect anyone's peace," Muhammad claimed.

leadership roles within the movement fractured the Nation into different sects that threatened not only to pull apart the religious organization but also to endanger Elijah Muhammad's life. Realizing this, the Messenger fled from Chicago, leaving behind his wife, Clara, and their family, which had now grown to five children. His departure marked the first time since he had married that Muhammad was separated from his family for any length of time.

The Nation's leader spent most of the next seven years as an itinerant preacher spreading the teachings of the movement. He ranged from the Midwest to the East Coast and then down to the South, returning periodically to Chicago to check up on his family and supporters. During this period, he lived like a fugitive, using an alias wherever he went.

Among Muhammad's stops was Washington, D.C., where he rented a room under the name of Mr. Boguns. For three days, he remained in his room, refraining from food and drink. When the home-owner, a man who later became known as Benjamin X, invited him to dinner the following day, Muhammad went out and bought some food for the entire family. This marked the beginning of one of his rituals: the communal meal, during which religious lessons were held.

During such meals, Muhammad would talk to his disciples about the Bible, which, as the son of a Baptist minister, he knew extremely well. Gradually, he would reveal the fallacy of the white man's Christian tale. "The Bible is their graveyard," he said of blacks, "and they must awaken from it."

In discussing the Bible, Muhammad liked to ask his listeners rhetorical questions. What kind of God would allow the trauma of slavery, or the violence that tears at black lives? Muhammad himself had traveled all over America, and he saw blacks in misery everywhere he went. They were cold in the winter and hungry in the summer. How long did they have to wait for scraps off the white man's table? What kind of God would treat his people with such contempt?

The answer was simple: a white man's God. "Christianity," Muhammad said, "is one of the most perfect black-slave making religions on our planet. It has completely killed the so-called Negroes' mentality." He noted ironically that the martyrdom of Jesus Christ held special meaning to the black race. Whites did not suffer; it was blacks who paid for the white man's sins. Muhammad told his disciples that his god was Allah, a god not only of peace but of righteousness and dignity. People who worshiped Allah would become fearless and receive divine protection from the evil white devils.

Muhammad's vision of the human race was indeed apocalyptic. Everything he taught was aimed at preparing blacks for the end of the world. In the great holy war between Allah and the devil that would occur on Judgment Day, the world would be destroyed and only a select few would remain.

A conflict of a different sort than the one Muhammad was predicting took hold in December 1941: the United States entered World War II. Maintaining that Black Muslims were forbidden to bear arms or perform acts of violence unless directed by Allah, Muhammad refused to register for the military draft. On May 8, 1942, during a meeting at a private home, he was arrested by federal agents for failing to register. At the time, Muhammad was just 5 months short of his 45th birthday—the age when a person was no longer required to participate in military service.

A short time after his arrest, Muhammad was convicted on two counts: failing to take part in the draft and encouraging others to evade it. He received a sentence of five years and was sent to the Federal Correctional Institution at Milan, Michigan. "The devil cooked up the charges," he later declared, adding that he had been "tried and imprisoned for teaching my people the truth about themselves." Many of Muhammad's male followers, including two of his sons, were also arrested for draft evasion.

There were other problems as well. The Black Muslims—thanks to a lobbyist in Chicago who was trying to win black support for America's enemy in the Pacific, Japan—were suspected of siding with the Japanese in the war. The Federal Bureau of Investigation (FBI) put the Chicago temple under surveillance, and a subsequent raid on the temple by FBI agents yielded a cache of weapons and additional arrests. "It should now be clear," Muhammad said, "that the attacks made upon us by the brutal American police forces with FBI harassment and persecution, that Allah has manifested the white race of America to be nothing but a race of devils."

While Muhammad and the others languished in prison, the burden of keeping the Nation going fell on the shoulders of Black Muslim women. They collected iron, paper, and other items and sold them to help keep the Nation afloat financially. Sister Clara, who became especially active in the running of the Chicago temple, corresponded regularly with her husband and visited him in prison. Through her efforts, Muhammad was able to maintain contact with the movement.

The first months at the federal prison in Milan, Michigan, were difficult ones for Muhammad and his sons. Prison officials, unfamiliar with the beliefs of Black Muslims, made no allowances for their daily customs, such as praying five times a day. The prisoners' dietary practices also proved problematic. Black Muslims were expressly forbidden to eat corn bread and pork because these items were the food of slaves. Moreover, they were allowed to eat other meats only if they were fresh. Such dietary restrictions

Black Muslim women await the beginning of a court hearing that involved three Chi-
cago-based Nation of Islam leaders in late 1942. Women took a more active role in
running the movement during World War II, when many of the Nation's male followers were imprisoned for refusing to fulfill their U.S. military service obligations.

were difficult to adhere to in prison, where most meals included some pork or lard.

In 1943, after six months in prison, Muhammad and other Black Muslims managed to convince the authorities that they were sincere in their religious practices. Consequently, their special requirements were accommodated. Showing the depth of their religious commitment had yet another effect: Prison authorities began to entrust Black Muslims with important tasks. Muhammad, who won the respect of inmates and guards alike, was made an orderly of the guards' quarters.

Every evening, after their prison jobs and classes had ended, Muhammad conducted seminars for his followers and tried to win over new disciples. In addition to teaching these inmates English, history, and numerology (the study of the hidden significance of numbers), he discussed the creation of man, as revealed by Wallace Fard, and gave an account of the black man's traumatic loss of his African identity and culture. Muhammad traced for his listeners the history of the Black Muslims, from their enslavement in West Africa to their lives as slaves in the United States. By providing the inmates with a link to the past, he hoped to give them a sense of pride in who they were. Like Marcus Garvey, he was keen to have his followers think of themselves as belonging to a group.

Muhammad sometimes highlighted his lessons by drawing on a blackboard. On one side, he sketched a faceless lynch victim under an American flag; on the other side, he drew the Islamic emblems of a star and crescent. Underneath these images, he wrote, "Freedom or Death?" Muhammad then recounted the brutal South of his childhood, telling them about the remarkable scene of racial violence that he witnessed at an early age. He claimed on some occasions that it was his father who had been lynched.

When indoctrinating new disciples into the Nation of Islam, Muhammad always included an apocalyptic message about the impending destruction of the earth. He said that Allah, in the form of Wallace Fard, had told him how the end of the world would occur. Hovering over the earth was an enormous wheel, called the Mother of Planes, that was the size of a small planet. On Judgment Day, the wheel would destroy the earth by emitting fire and poison gas. Muhammad described this deadly object in the following manner:

> The Great Wheel which many of us see in the sky today is not so much a wheel as one may think in such terms, but rather a place made like a wheel. . . . [It] is one-half mile by a half mile and is the largest mechanical man-made object in the sky. It carries fifteen hundred bombing planes with the most deadliest explosives—the type used in bringing up mountains on the earth. . . . The bombs are equipped with motors and the toughest of steel was used in making them. This steel drills and takes the bombs into the earth at a depth of one mile. . . . This is only one of the things in store for the white man's evil world. This is to warn you and me to fly to our own God and people.

Muhammad was quick to point out that Allah was not without compassion. There would be 8 to 10 days' advance notice of the world's destruction. The Mother of Planes would drop pamphlets written in Arabic and English. A siren in the sky would serve as a signal that the end of the world was drawing near. Exactly 144,000 blacks would be spared. They, in turn, would usher in a new era of black dominion.

Muhammad maintained that the destruction of the earth would occur before the year 2000. He suggested that 1970 might very well be the year of the apocalypse, although the exact date was known only to Allah. In the meantime, all blacks should follow the teachings of Allah and prepare themselves for Judgment Day. That was the only way they could be

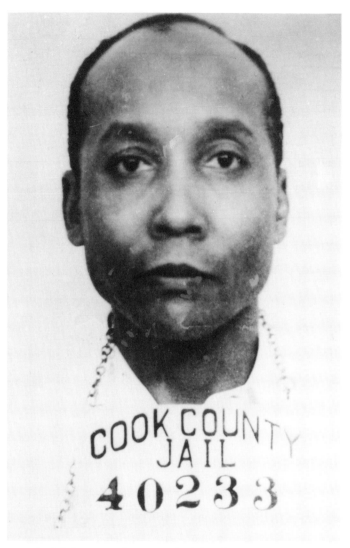

A mug shot of Muhammad at the age of 44, after he was convicted of draft evasion and encouraging others to resist the draft. He wound up spending nearly four years at the federal prison in Milan, Michigan.

saved. Muhammad counseled his listeners, "We the black people of the earth are number one owners of it, the best of all human beings. You are the Most Powerful, the Most Beautiful and the Wisest."

Embracing the Nation of Islam brought the inmates physical as well as spiritual release. Always properly behaved, the Black Muslims frequently saw their sentences reduced. Muhammad won his release in 1946 and returned immediately to Chicago.

Back with his family after being, as he put it, "deprived of a father's love for his family" for nearly four years, Muhammad resumed his role as leader of the Nation. The many years that he had spent in flight and in prison showed other Black Muslims how devoted he was to their cause and cemented his claim to the movement's leadership. He began to compare himself to the persecuted prophets of the Bible and Koran, and thus he became known as the supreme prophet of Allah. **◀▶**

6

SPREADING
THE WORD

WHILE SERVING TIME in prison, Elijah Muhammad realized that most black churches and civil rights organizations lacked well-developed social programs for the downtrodden. As a result, after he was released from the Federal Correctional Institution at Milan, Michigan, in 1946, he shifted the focus of the Nation of Islam to helping the needy and giving direction to their lives. Backed by the Nation, he offered food and work to the outcast and the unemployed—particularly to juvenile delinquents, prostitutes, and former convicts—and helped drug addicts overcome their dependence on narcotics.

The results were astounding. By providing these people with spiritual guidance, the Nation succeeded in improving thousands of lives. And the movement often gained new converts as a result. Membership in the Nation rose from a few thousand in the mid-1940s to approximately 80,000 over the next decade and a half, with the largest increase coming in the late 1950s.

As the number of Black Muslims grew, Muhammad began to search in Chicago for a larger temple. A building on East 34th Street, which had formerly served as an animal hospital, was chosen for the headquarters. A neon sign proclaiming Muhammad's Holy Temple of Islam and an Islamic crescent were placed on top of the building.

Housed along with the temple was a school. Religious meetings were held in the building three eve-

A photograph of Muhammad appears on the front page of Muhammad Speaks, a newspaper established in 1961 to spread the message of the Nation of Islam. Initially printed in a Chicago basement, the periodical eventually became the largest-circulation black publication in the country.

nings a week. On the other nights classes were held for both youths, such as the Muslim Girls' Training Class, and adults, most notably the Fruit of Islam.

Although Muhammad was kept busy with his teaching, organizing, and preaching duties, he also found time to start a business. In the summer of 1947, he opened a combined grocery, bakery, and restaurant at 3117 South Wentworth. The grocery and bakery sold solely those items that fell within the Muslims' strict dietary code. The menu at the restaurant featured only the simple, natural ingredients approved by the Nation. Muhammad's daughters Ethel and Lotte worked as cooks and bakers; his sons worked as dishwashers and delivery boys and handled other chores. The business was one of the first ventures to realize Fard's dream of economic independence for blacks.

By not spending money on alcohol, tobacco, gambling, and other vices, members of the Nation were expected to be able to contribute 10 percent of their income to the movement. The rest of their income, according to Muhammad, should be put toward helping blacks.

By following this program, the Nation worked economic miracles. A survey of Black Muslims in Detroit during the Great Depression revealed that during the early 1930s most of them were on public welfare or received some other form of financial assistance and lived in the ghetto. By 1937, however, the majority of Black Muslims held jobs and were better off financially than other blacks. Most of them no longer lived in the inner city, although they continued to hold meetings there. Although this upward mobility was due in part to the revival of the American economy, it also demonstrated the fruits of their disciplined way of life. There were even more prosperous times in the years ahead.

Economic security, according to Black Muslims, depended on five key points:

1. Recognize the necessity for unity and group operation (activities).

2. Pool your resources, physically as well as financially.

3. Stop wanton criticism of everything that is black-owned and black-operated.

4. Keep in mind—Jealousy Destroys from Within.

5. Observe the operations of the white man. He is successful. He makes no excuses for his failures. He works hard in a collective manner. You do the same.

One of the central aims of the Nation of Islam has been to educate its followers, including these students at the University of Islam in Chicago. "We must educate ourselves and our children into the rich power of knowledge," Muhammad said, "which has elevated every people who have sought and used it."

The financial success of the Black Muslims made their movement more attractive to prospective new-comers. During the late 1940s, most of the converts to the Nation were rural southerners who had just moved north and found themselves in situations no better than those who had migrated to the cities before World War I. Poor and uneducated, the ma-jority of these people lacked the skills that were needed for employment in the North. Still making the transition from a rural life to an urban one, they were out of step not only with white employers but with urban black communities, which resented their intrusion into established neighborhoods. "The un-wanted from Dixie," a Chicago journalist called them.

There was one person who wanted these migrants, though, and he was Elijah Muhammad. The Nation counseled them on everything from their personal habits and relationships to how to save money by

In the early 1950s, Malcolm X, a former street hustler and petty criminal, emerged as Muham-mad's prized pupil and chief spokesman. He was eventually appointed by Muhammad as na-tional minister of the Nation of Islam.

avoiding the vices in the cities. Muhammad taught them to keep a tight rein over their finances. "Stop wasting your money!" he said to them. "Your money was not given to you, so why should you give it away for what you can do without? We could save millions of dollars for education, land, machines, cattle, homes, and factories. How can we begin? Stop spending money for tobacco, dope, cigarettes, whiskey, fine clothes, fine automobiles, expensive rugs and carpets, idleness, sport and gambling. Stop living on credit and loans. We must build a better future for ourselves and our children."

One of the people who was drawn to the Nation's teachings was Malcolm Little, a black inmate at Norfolk State Prison in Massachusetts. His brothers Reginald and Philbert and sister Hilda had already joined the Nation of Islam, and in 1948 Reginald tried to get Malcolm to become a member. "I'll show you how to get out of prison," Reginald promised, but only if Malcolm would listen to some brotherly advice.

The first thing Reginald told Malcolm was to abstain from eating pork and smoking cigarettes. In time, brother taught brother more and more about the teachings of the Nation. "The white man is the devil," Reginald said. "The black man is brainwashed." For Malcolm Little, who had spent his entire 23 years without much direction, these words made sense. Most of the hardship he had suffered could be attributed to whites.

Born in Omaha, Nebraska, in 1925 and raised in East Lansing, Michigan, Little had experienced a childhood that was filled with scenes of racial violence. His father was a Baptist minister and active Garveyite who carried out his religious and black nationalist activities in spite of threats on his life. He was murdered, most likely by white supremacists, when Malcolm was six years old.

Malcolm Little eventually became a ward of the state. Despite showing great intellectual promise in school, he possessed an unstoppable fury that landed him in a juvenile detention center by the age of 13. A few years later, he moved to the black ghettos of Boston and New York, where he sank into a life of petty thievery and drug dealing. When the police hauled him from the streets in 1945, he was still a wildly angry, antisocial young man whose perverse pride in being an outcast earned him the nickname of Satan among his fellow inmates.

The Nation gave Little the hammer to pound out his rage. It was the white man who had caused him to live like an animal on the streets. By embracing the Nation and directing his anger at the corrupt white race, he also became able—for the first time in his life—to speak of love and forgiveness.

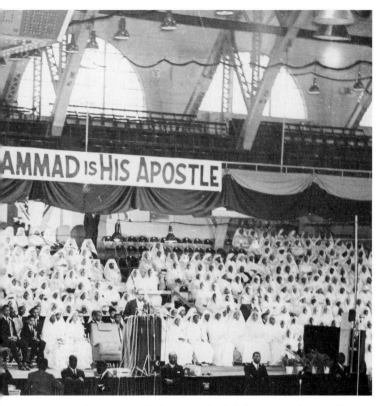

A national convention of the Nation of Islam. The yearly meeting is always held on February 26, Wallace Fard's birthday.

Little proceeded to study Muhammad's teachings with a zeal that he would display for many years to come. He worked tirelessly to improve his oral and writing skills, spending hour upon hour in the prison library poring over religious, historical, philosophical, and spiritual books. To the amazement of the Norfolk Prison authorities, he changed his attitude toward the other inmates and guards from open hostility to courteous respect. Next, he informed the prison officials that he had dropped his slave name of Little and had replaced it with the letter X. From now on, he would be known as Malcolm X.

Among Malcolm X's other acts was to write a letter to Elijah Muhammad in which he expressed his profound passion for his newfound faith. Muhammad answered the letter promptly. The Nation's leader welcomed his new charge into the fold and told him that the black prisoner symbolized white society's crimes of keeping black men oppressed, deprived, and ignorant, of turning them into criminals. Muhammad enclosed with his response a five-dollar bill, a habitual gesture of goodwill toward prisoners who joined the Nation.

Malcolm X's faith received a severe test in the early 1950s, when his brother Reginald was expelled from the Nation because of adultery. Word had gotten out that Reginald was having an affair with a secretary in New York's Temple Number Seven, which led Muhammad to order Reginald to leave the movement. Looking to put things right, Malcolm X wrote a letter in defense of his brother and mailed it to Muhammad.

"What could make you doubt the truth other than your own weak self?" Muhammad responded. "If you once believed the truth, and now you are beginning to doubt the truth, then you didn't believe the truth in the first place." Advising Malcolm X that the correct decision had been made about his brother, Muhammad urged the inmate to forget about the matter and continue with his studies. Malcolm X did exactly what the Nation's leader suggested.

In August 1952, Malcolm X's exemplary behavior won him an early release from prison. He headed immediately for Detroit, where he moved in with his brother Wilfred and became active in the operation of Temple Number One, which had been established by Wallace Fard and Muhammad nearly 20 years earlier. One thing left Malcolm X puzzled, however. He did not understand why the temple was never crowded during prayer meetings. That situation would soon change, as it became Malcolm X's responsibility to fill up those empty seats.

Shortly after he settled in Michigan, Malcolm X went to Chicago to hear Muhammad preach. The new recruit was practically overcome by the awe he

Muhammad backed by his protégé, Malcolm X. "My worship of him was so awesome," Malcolm X said of the Nation of Islam leader, "that he was the first man whom I had ever feared—not fear such as of a man with a gun, but the fear such as one has of the power of the sun."

felt in the presence of the man who was said to be the Messenger of Allah. Muhammad was likewise struck by this bright, young protégé. Yet the Nation's leader also wondered how long Malcolm X would remain pious now that he was out of prison. After all, he had previously been a thief, a drug dealer, and a pimp, and the world was still full of temptation.

In formally introducing Malcolm X to the members of Temple Number Two, Muhammad told them that when God bragged how faithful Job was, the devil argued that only God's protective hedge around Job kept him so. Remove the hedge, the devil suggested, and Job will curse his maker. "Well, now, our good brother Malcolm's hedge is removed and we will see how he does," Muhammad said. "I believe that he is going to remain faithful."

Muhammad's faith in Malcolm X was quickly rewarded. After religious services were held one Sunday, the Black Muslim leader invited Malcolm X to dinner in the old mansion that the Nation had recently purchased in Hyde Park, a dilapidated neighborhood in Chicago's South Side ghetto. Muhammad's sons had cleared the land around the house, which had once been used as a garbage dump, and had begun to renovate its 18 rooms.

At dinner, Malcolm X hung on to Muhammad's every word. During a pause in the conversation, the young man got up the nerve to bring to Muhammad's attention the dwindling number of followers attending Temple Number One in Detroit. Muhammad, sensing Malcolm's dynamism, agreed that it was a problem and urged him to recruit new members. "Go after the young people," he said. "Once you get them, the older ones will follow through shame."

Malcolm X took these words to heart. He began to speak to blacks in Detroit's bars, poolrooms, and street corners. Carried away by his need to reach the souls of other blacks and make them see the power and beauty of the black race, he talked to them until he was hoarse. After only a few months, he managed to triple the membership of Temple Number One. He would win thousands of other converts in the ensuing years.

Thurgood Marshall, then the chief legal counsel for the NAACP, quipped that the Nation was "run by a bunch of thugs organized from prisons and jails and financed, I am sure, by [Egyptian president Gamal

Abdel] Nasser or some Arab group." In one sense, Marshall was not far off base: the Nation saw inmates convert to the Black Muslim religion in droves. "When the Black Man who is a hardened criminal hears the teachings of Mr. Muhammad, immediately he makes an about-face," Malcolm X explained. "Where the warden couldn't straighten him out through solitary confinement, as soon as he became a Muslim, he begins to become a model prisoner right in that institution, far more than whites or so-called Negroes who confess Christianity."

In 1953, Malcolm X was rewarded for his successful work as a recruiter by being appointed assistant minister of Temple Number One. A gifted and charismatic speaker, he often displayed a barbed wit. "Yes, I'm an extremist," he would tell his listeners. "The black race in America is in extremely bad condition."

Yet Malcolm X constantly wanted to learn more about being an effective speaker, and so he tried to spend as much time as possible with his mentor, who had a penchant for speaking in parables. Malcolm X often accompanied Muhammad on his rounds of Black Muslim groceries, whose number had multiplied over the previous few years. The two men frequently engaged in theological discussions as they swept the grocery floors or organized the inventory.

Muhammad liked to teach his gifted pupil by telling him stories that had a moral. One day, he showed Malcolm X a dirty glass, then placed it on a counter beside a clean one. "You want to know how to spread my teachings?" Muhammad asked. "Don't condemn if you see a person has a dirty glass of water, just show them the clean glass of water that you have. When they inspect it, you won't have to say that yours is better."

Malcolm X never forgot his teacher's words, although he admitted he sometimes found it difficult to heed Muhammad's advice. "Of all the things that

Several Harlemites study the Messenger, *a periodical that helped spread the teachings of the Black Muslim movement. By the late 1950s, the Nation of Islam had grown so large that it began to attract the attention of the national media.*

Mr. Muhammad ever was to teach me," Malcolm X later said, "I don't know why, that still stands out in my mind. Although I haven't always practiced it. I love too much to battle. I'm inclined to tell somebody if his glass of water is dirty."

Muhammad asked Malcolm X to leave Detroit in 1953 and live in Chicago for a while so he could begin his training as a minister. Ministers were already in place in the Nation's other temples; Muhammad planned for Malcolm X to go from temple to temple and increase the movement's membership at each stop. After months of intensive training, Muhammad sent Malcolm X to Boston to organize Temple Number Eleven. After he succeeded there, Malcolm X moved on to Philadelphia and Temple Number Twelve. His unquestioning devotion to the teachings of Muhammad, combined with his articulate anger at the black man's condition, inspired old members and new converts everywhere he went.

With a successful track record, Malcolm X was appointed minister of New York's Temple Number Seven, little more than a storefront, in June 1954. He helped it grow in size, then moved on to Springfield, Massachusetts, where he opened Temple Number Thirteen, and Hartford, Connecticut, where he founded Temple Number Fourteen.

During this period, Malcolm X still returned to Chicago to visit Muhammad; the Messenger remained his chief source of inspiration. Occasionally, Malcolm X expressed his impatience with the slowly increasing size of the Nation. Muhammad, who sometimes introduced Malcolm X to audiences as "the angriest black man in America," would calm him by saying, "Most people seeing a man in an old touring car going real slow think the man doesn't want to go fast, but the man knows that to drive any faster would destroy the old car. When he gets a fast car, then he will drive at a fast speed." When Malcolm complained about the ineffectiveness of some of the ministers, Muhammad admonished him: "I would rather have a mule I can depend upon than a race horse that I can't depend upon."

The tremendous growth of the Nation continued through 1955, when 15 more temples were established across the country. That December, Muhammad and his followers also purchased a synagogue and school at 5335 South Greenwood Avenue in Chicago. The building, which contained classrooms, offices, a small library, and an auditorium, became the movement's largest facility.

By the end of the decade, the Nation had 50 temples in operation. Not surprisingly, the Nation's economic programs expanded as membership increased. As more and more Black Muslim businesses opened up, Muhammad and his sons Herbert and

By the end of the 1950s, the Nation of Islam had established 50 temples nationwide, including a new Temple Number Two (right) and the University of Islam (left). These structures were erected across the street from the Nation's headquarters, a refurbished mansion on Chicago's South Side, where Muhammad lived with his family.

Elijah, Jr., launched a back-to-the-farm program to stimulate interest in owning land. Their father believed that whites had convinced blacks to settle for jobs as janitors and elevator operators rather than to aspire to being self-sufficient farmers. "Build black, buy black" was Muhammad's advice to his followers.

The small-business efforts of the Black Muslims eventually expanded into grocery stores, apartment buildings, factories, farms, cleaning establishments, restaurants, bakeries, and service shops for office machines and venetian blind repairs. At one point during the 1950s, the combined wealth of these Black Muslim enterprises was estimated at $10 million. By 1960, the Nation owned a half million dollars' worth of real estate in the Chicago area alone.

To spread the word about Black Muslims, Muhammad regularly wrote a column for the *Pittsburgh Courier*, which was the largest-circulation black newspaper in America. Boasting more than 300,000 readers, the paper published news about the activities and programs of the Nation. Although the column proved to be a success, when the paper was sold to more conservative owners Muhammad's features were discontinued. He subsequently wrote a column for the *Los Angeles Herald-Dispatch*. Then, in 1961, the movement began to publish its own newspaper, *Muhammad Speaks*. A weekly periodical, it eventually became the largest black publication in the country, with a circulation of half a million. ◆

7

"WE DEMAND COMPLETE SEPARATION"

◄◊►

THE BLACK MUSLIMS took a giant step onto the national stage in the summer of 1959, when journalist Mike Wallace narrated a television documentary called "The Hate That Produced Hate." The program revealed the core of Elijah Muhammad's white-man-as-devil theology and shocked most white Americans, who had not realized the extreme degree of discontent among blacks. Prior to the airing of the documentary, churches readily rented out their halls to Black Muslims for meetings. But after network television had spread the news of the movement's volatile separatist doctrine, it became much harder for the Nation of Islam to obtain accommodations.

By the end of the 1950s, the views of the Black Muslims helped threaten to rip apart the social fabric of the country at its seams. Liberal whites and black integrationists were busy supporting the moderate forms of civil rights protest launched by the Reverend Martin Luther King, Jr., who in 1957 had founded the Southern Christian Leadership Conference with Bayard Rustin and others to challenge racial segregation in public facilities. Roy Wilkins, executive

Black Muslims picket in front of New York City's Criminal Courts Building in January 1963. They were protesting the trial of two Nation of Islam members who were charged with assault and attempted riot while selling copies of Muhammad Speaks.

secretary of the NAACP, released an official statement in July 1959 that lambasted Muhammad's radical stance: "For years the NAACP has been opposed
to white extremists preaching hatred of Negro people,
and we are equally opposed to Negro extremists
preaching against white people simply for the sake of
whiteness."

Nevertheless, Black Muslims remained adamantly
opposed to desegregation and were insulted by the

Racial segregation in the nation's public schools was a major concern during the early stages of the civil rights movement. Although the United States Supreme Court ruled in 1954, in the case of Brown v. Board of Education of Topeka, that segregating schoolchildren by race is unconstitutional, it took years to dismantle the system of separate schools—and even longer to overcome massive resistance among whites. Jefferson Thomas (right), one of nine black teenagers to gain admittance in 1957 to Central High School in Litle Rock, Arkansas, was among those who continued to be harassed by whites.

Christian philosophy of turning the other cheek. It was inconceivable to them that whites would share with blacks the advantages and privileges of their position. Even more to the point, living in an integrated society with the ancestors of slave owners was one of the Black Muslims' darkest nightmares.

According to the Nation, men such as King were leading the black masses astray by lobbying for integration. Muhammad said pointedly of King, "The dog wants something to eat [from his master] while there is plenty of meat for the dog in the bushes out there, if he would go out and hunt for it."

Black Muslims viewed integration as a last-ditch attempt by whites to save themselves from the looming destruction of the earth that Muhammad had said might occur in 1970. For a black to live alongside whites meant certain contamination. "Today's world is floating in corruption," Muhammad said. "Its complete disintegration is both imminent and inescapable. Any man who integrates with the world must share in its disintegration and destruction. If the Black man would listen, he need not be a part of this certain doom."

Among those whom Muhammad regarded as doomed was James Meredith, who was denied admission to the University of Mississippi in 1961 because of his race. Backed by the U.S. Supreme Court, he became the first black to be admitted to the university. It took more than 3,000 federal troops, however, to assure his safety in the classroom.

Muhammad spoke out against this example of integration. "I wouldn't want the Army to think about coming to help me against the white man, to allow me to come into his house or in the school or his restaurant," he said. "If you tell me, 'I don't want you here,' that's sufficient. I'm gone."

Ironically, the separatist theology of the Black Muslims attracted some of the same people who, under different circumstances, might have menaced them with a hangman's noose. George Lincoln Rockwell, head of the American Nazi party, a white supremacist group, attended a Black Muslim rally in Washington, D.C., to offer his support against racially mixed marriages. Muhammad had already made his position on interracial marriage quite clear. "What do we want to marry a white woman for?" he asked. "The very desire there is ignorant and evil.

It's against divine law for either side to integrate in such a way."

As the 1960s progressed, Muhammad began to speak of a separate state for blacks within the United States, just as Wallace Fard had done years earlier. The Black Muslim leader stated in a 1963 interview with the *New York Times*, "The Negro must think in terms of bettering himself, and this he can only do by thinking in terms of his own black civilization." If black Americans could not go back to Africa, as Marcus Garvey had suggested, then they should be granted their own homeland in the United States.

A marriage of opposites: George Lincoln Rockwell (center, with pipe) prepares to lead an anti-black rally held by the American Nazi party, a white supremacist group whose doctrine of racial separatism mirrored, strangely enough, the Nation of Islam's own separatist views. On one occasion, Rockwell attended a Black Muslim rally to show his support for the Nation's opposition to mixed marriages.

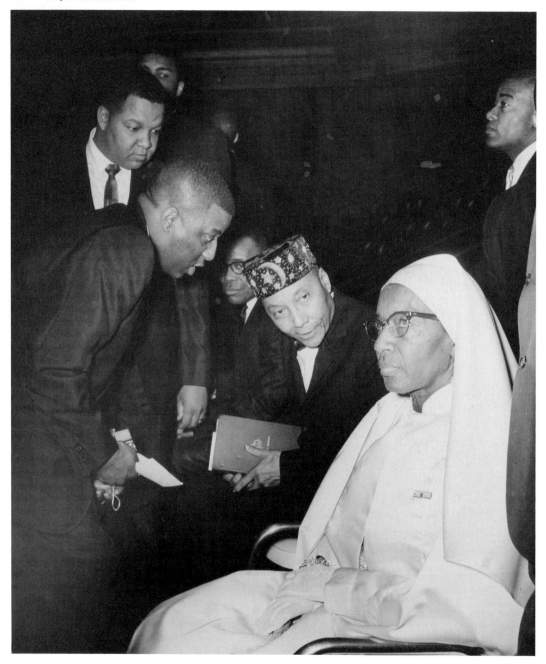

Muhammad looks to his wife, Clara, during a Black Muslim convention in 1965. John Ali (foreground), the Nation of Islam's minister of public relations, was among those who attempted to wrest control of the movement when Muhammad decided to take a less active role in the Nation's daily affairs.

"We believe that our former slave-masters are obligated to maintain and supply our needs in this separate territory for the next 20 to 25 years—until we are able to produce and supply our own needs," Muhammad said. "Since we cannot get along with them in peace and equality . . . we . . . demand . . . complete separation." When slavery was legally abolished in 1865, there had been some discussion of freed slaves receiving 40 acres and a mule as compensation for the injustice they had been forced to suffer. Nearly 100 years later, Muhammad was maintaining that blacks had yet to shake off the yoke of slavery.

There were other shackles to discard as well. In the early 1960s, prison authorities denied Black Muslims the right to practice their religion behind bars. Some of the inmates protested, and two of their cases were eventually heard by the U.S. Supreme Court. In one of the suits, 10 Black Muslim inmates in California claimed that the removal of their religious books violated the Fourteenth Amendment, which guarantees freedom of religion. In the other case, three Black Muslims in a New York prison accused the authorities of violating the Civil Rights Act of 1871, which maintains that all people may worship their chosen religion without interference from the state. The Supreme Court ruled in both cases that it was "constitutionally permissible" for Black Muslims to be denied the right to practice their religion because their theology threatened national security.

The federal government decided to take an even more pronounced step toward protecting the American public from the Nation when it began to keep track of the movement's members. The Fruit of Islam, the Nation's highly trained paramilitary corps, particularly worried government officials, who surmised that Muhammad was amassing a small but effective army. Its members' telephones were wiretapped; their personal activities were closely monitored by the FBI.

Before long, blacks began to complain that one visit to a Black Muslim temple was enough of a reason for them to be placed under FBI surveillance. Muhammad shrewdly pointed out that the FBI could "catch all the lynchers and school bombers in the South" with a fraction of the agents assigned to watch him. Malcolm X claimed that no fewer than 15 FBI agents watched Temple Number Seven, his main headquarters.

Malcolm X, however, gave the authorities plenty of reasons to worry. His public-speaking style had grown more flamboyant and increasingly militant over the years. He often alluded in his speeches to violence and destruction, telling his listeners such things as "You don't stick a knife in a man's back nine inches and pull it out six inches and say you're making progress" and "Like Samson, I am ready to pull down the white man's temple."

Always smartly dressed in a dark suit and narrow tie, like the model businessman, Malcolm X was indeed an imposing figure. Reporters and television crews flocked to him whenever they wanted a comment by the Black Muslims. On those occasions, Malcolm X would persist in advising the media to talk directly to Muhammad—sometimes he would even supply them with photographs of the Messenger—yet the newsmen kept on coming back to Malcolm X because he was much more colorful. His rhetoric was so spellbinding, in fact, that he became one of the most popular lecturers on the college circuit. The young clergyman embodied the nation's conception of the angry face of black America.

In 1962, Malcolm X found himself even closer to the center of the limelight: Muhammad appointed him national minister of the Nation. The Messenger was then 65 years old and was suffering from chronic asthma and bronchitis. On the advice of his doctor, he bought a modest two-bedroom house in Phoenix, Arizona, to serve as a winter retreat.

Almost as soon as Muhammad, along with his family and three aides, moved away from Chicago, discord broke out among Malcolm X; John Ali, the Nation's head of public relations; Raymond Sharieff, the leader of the Fruit of Islam; and the other officers Muhammad had put in charge of the Black Muslims and their multimillion-dollar businesses. During the next few years, an epic struggle for control of the movement would threaten to fracture the Nation from within. ✺

8

THE CHICKENS COME HOME TO ROOST

BITTER RIVALRIES WITHIN the Nation of Islam grew more pronounced in April 1962, when a group of Black Muslims in Los Angeles confronted the local police. The encounter left one Nation member dead and a dozen more wounded. Malcolm X responded to the violence by saying that Black Muslims should retaliate in kind against the police. The other leaders of the Nation wanted to avoid further trouble with the authorities, however, and permitted him to do nothing other than make angry speeches.

In his public addresses, Malcolm X had already been focusing on political matters instead of religious issues for some time. To give him less of a voice in the movement, he was stripped of his responsibilities as editor of *Muhammad Speaks*, and Elijah Muhammad's son Herbert ordered the newspaper's staff to limit its coverage of Malcolm X's activities. A short time later, the national minister was told by the Messenger to stop appearing on network television news broadcasts.

The rift continued into 1963, when two of Muhammad's former secretaries, both in their twenties, filed paternity suits against the Nation's leader, claiming that the 67-year-old Muhammad had fathered their 4 children. In an attempt to uncover the truth, Malcolm X interviewed the two women. They not only provided him with evidence to support their

"Love yourself and your kind," Muhammad counseled his followers. "Let us refrain from doing evil to each other, and let us love each other as brothers, as we are the same flesh and blood. . . . It is a fool who does not love himself and his people. Your black skin is the best, and never try changing its color."

93

A shotgun-wielding plainclothes police officer stands guard over three handcuffed Black Muslims on a Los Angeles street in April 1962, after a brawl between Nation of Islam members and the police got out of hand and resulted in the slaying of one of Muhammad's followers. The incident ultimately helped widen the rift between Malcolm X, who wanted to respond to the confrontation with violence, and the other Nation leaders, who wanted to avoid any more trouble with the authorities.

claims but told him Muhammad had become convinced that Malcolm X was turning against him.

These revelations deeply shook the dynamic young minister's faith in his mentor. Still, Malcolm X decided to hear Muhammad out, and so he made a trip to the older man's home in Phoenix. Side by side, the two ministers walked around Muhammad's swimming pool. Malcolm X listened closely as Muhammad drew on biblical parables comparing himself with King David and Noah, who had also suffered moral lapses, to justify his own behavior. Muhammad did not deny the charges that had been leveled against him, Malcolm X noticed. Consequently, his faith in the movement began to wane.

What might be construed as the kiss of death between the two men occurred later in 1963. At a rally in Philadelphia, Muhammad embraced Malcolm X in front of the assembly and told the crowd, "This is my most faithful, hardworking minister. He will follow me until he dies." That embrace marked the last time they were ever seen together in public.

Malcolm X replaced his loss of faith in Muhammad's moral authority by channeling his energies into black nationalist activities. On August 28, 1963, nearly a quarter million demonstrators participated in the March on Washington for Jobs and Freedom that A. Philip Randolph and Bayard Rustin organized in the nation's capital. The day was filled with a parade of people singing hymns as they marched from the Washington Monument to the Lincoln Memorial; it culminated in a series of powerful speeches in support of civil rights. Martin Luther King, Jr., who was the last speaker of the day, called the massive protest an attempt "to arouse the conscience of the nation over the economic plight of the Negro."

Malcolm X had quite a different reaction to the day's events. "I don't believe we're going to overcome [by] singing," he told reporters. "If you're going to get yourself a .45 and start singing 'We Shall Overcome,' I'm with you." More and more, the barrel of a gun seemed to him the only means for making white America take notice of its black citizens.

Such incendiary comments kept Malcolm X in the bad graces of the Nation. Finally, things came to a climax. Following the assassination of President John F. Kennedy on November 22, 1963, Malcolm X told the press that he believed the hate in whites had not stopped at the killing of blacks but had spread unchecked until it had finally struck down the country's head of state. Malcolm X's public response to Kennedy's slaying was "The chickens [have] come home to roost."

Malcolm X's callous comment resulted in a summons to Phoenix, where Muhammad reprimanded him. "That was very ill timed," the Nation's leader said. "A statement like that can make it hard on Muslims in general. I have to silence you for the next ninety days—so that Muslims everywhere can disassociate themselves from the blunder." In view of their deteriorating relationship, Malcolm X's unpopular statement about Kennedy may very well have served as a pretext for Muhammad to check the power of his chief spokesman.

To regain Muhammad's favor, Malcolm X journeyed to Miami, Florida, in February 1964 to meet with Cassius Clay, a popular boxer who had just secretly converted to Islam and changed his name to Muhammad Ali. The 28-year-old minister believed that by convincing Ali to associate himself with the Nation, the movement would gain a lot of positive publicity and might restore Elijah Muhammad's confidence in his chief minister along with it. Ali publicly acknowledged his conversion on February 26, the day after he won the heavyweight title in a match against Sonny Liston. As time wore on, Ali would prove to be a generous friend to the Black Muslims, donating a substantial amount of his earnings to the movement. Yet Malcolm X's fruitful visit with Ali did little to change Muhammad's attitude.

Malcolm X soon found out just how little. Toward the end of his 90-day suspension, several members of Harlem's Temple Number Seven said that a high-ranking Black Muslim had instructed them to assassinate Malcolm X. Their admission left the young clergyman stunned. "I felt like something in *nature* had failed—like the sun or the stars," he observed.

There could be only one response. In March 1964, Malcolm X announced that he was leaving the Nation to form a new organization, Muslim Mosque, Incorporated. Its charter members, totaling about 50 people, were former supporters of the Nation. Yet Malcolm X welcomed blacks of all religious denominations to join this militant group. Whites were also invited to contribute money and ideas.

The formation of a new Black Muslim organization enraged Muhammad and other Nation leaders. They branded Malcolm X a traitor and vilified him in *Muhammad Speaks.*

They soon had even more of a reason to regard Malcolm X as their enemy. Less than a month after he formed Muslim Mosque, Incorporated, he went on a spiritual pilgrimage to the holy city of Mecca. There he learned firsthand that a doctrine of black supremacy had no place in traditional Islam. Upon his return to the United States in late May, he told

Muhammad meets with civil rights leader Martin Luther King, Jr., in February 1966 to discuss what King called "the Negro's repellent slum life" in Chicago. Although the two men rarely agreed on the best way for blacks to win their civil rights, they both recognized a major problem facing Chicago's black population: segregated housing, which led to all-black, and invariably inferior, public schools.

"He has more intelligence in his little pinky than the rest of us have in our entire body," newly crowned heavyweight boxing champion Muhammad Ali (right) said of the man he called "his teacher," Elijah Muhammad. Ali brought a great deal of publicity to the Black Muslim movement by announcing his conversion to Islam on February 26, 1964, the day after he won the world title.

the press that he had been "spellbound by the graciousness I see displayed all around me by people of *all colors*" and proceeded to denounce the racist policies of the Nation: "For 12 long years I lived within the narrow-minded confines of the 'straight-jacket world' created by my strong belief Elijah Muhammad was a messenger direct from God Himself, and my faith in what I now see to be a pseudo-religious philosophy that he preaches."

Around this time, Muhammad's son Akbar, who was studying Islamic law at Al Azhar University in Cairo, Egypt, also broke ranks with the Nation. Akbar said of his father, "His concocted religious teachings are far from, and, in most cases, diametrically opposed to, Islam, and secondarily because of his politically sterile philosophy of the Afro-American struggle." Just one year earlier, Akbar had seen his brother Wallace and cousin Hasan Sharieff pushed out of the movement. "There are members of the top echelon in the movement who do not go along with [Elijah Muhammad]," Akbar maintained, "but they stay because they are getting good salaries."

Malcolm X kept the heat on the Nation. He insisted that Muhammad's movement had missed a great opportunity by failing to work with other civil rights organizations to find a better way of life for blacks. "Elijah spends his time denouncing white people and my followers," he said. "Why doesn't he denounce the Ku Klux Klan and the White Citizens Council? Why doesn't he send followers to Mississippi and Florida to help the Negro and white civil rights volunteers who are trying to better things there?" To accomplish these tasks, Malcolm X formed the Organization of Afro-American Unity (OAAU), a non-religious offshoot of Muslim Mosque, Incorporated.

As 1964 drew to an end, disciples of the Nation assaulted a number of Malcolm X's aides. Malcolm X himself was kept under surveillance by both the Nation and the FBI, leading him to suspect that they had organized a conspiracy against him. In December, he began to receive a series of death threats.

In early February 1965, a rumor popped up that the French government had uncovered a plot to kill Malcolm X while he was in Paris. In the middle of the month, his home in East Elmhurst, New York, was firebombed. He and his family barely managed to escape from their burning house. Then, barely a week later, on February 21, Malcolm X was gunned down by three men during a rally at the Audubon Ballroom in Harlem.

Talmadge Hayer, the only one of the three assassins to be arrested at the scene of the crime, denied having ties with the Nation. Muhammad and the Nation also disavowed having any involvement in

Early in the morning of February 23, 1965—just two days after Malcolm X was gunned down at the Audubon Ballroom in Harlem—his New York City headquarters, which had been located on the fourth floor of this building, was firebombed. Following these two incidents, Muhammad chose to keep the Nation of Islam out of the public eye.

Malcolm X's murder, although most observers thought otherwise and guessed that there would be a bloodbath between the rival factions. Indeed, these prophecies became a reality when mosques were burned in New York and San Francisco.

In Chicago, members of the Fruit of Islam armed themselves to protect the life of Muhammad, who described Malcolm X as "a star who had gone astray." The Nation's leader said that the slain minister "got what he preached" because he had urged blacks to arm themselves. The call to arms, Muhammad said, belongs to no one but Allah.

Eldridge Cleaver, who in 1967 became minister of information of the militant Black Panther party, a black nationalist group that did not shy away from using violence, maintained there was a time in the

1960s when most blacks thought about becoming Black Muslims. But by the end of the decade, the movement's powerful dominion over the black imagination had begun to wane. Filled with a growing sense of desperation, the nation's black ghettos had periodically erupted into destructive riots. Instead of trying to unify the different strands of black activists, Muhammad had chosen to keep the Nation out of the public spotlight.

Nevertheless, as the 1970s began, the Nation still claimed its share of followers. Muhammad continued to rule them from his house in Phoenix, which had now become his permanent residence. In a move

Members of the Nation of Islam carry Muhammad's coffin from the movement's Chicago temple on February 28, 1975. An estimated 10,000 followers attended the funeral service for the man who had guided the Nation for more than 40 years.

Muhammad's son Wallace finds himself riding a wave of support on March 4, 1975, after replacing his father as the head of the Nation of Islam. He later formed a splinter group of the Nation that welcomed people from all races as members.

befitting a powerful yet isolated man, he had his home monitored by closed-circuit cameras.

On August 12, 1972, Muhammad's wife, Clara, died at the age of 72. Ever since 1946, when her husband was released from prison, she had remained in the background, raising her children and acting as a role model for other Black Muslim women. In the years immediately following her death, Muhammad's public appearances remained few and far between.

When Muhammad finally emerged from isolation in 1974, he seemed to have experienced a change of heart. During one meeting, he said to his followers, "The slavemaster has given you all he could give you. He gave you freedom. Now get something for yourself." Instead of blaming whites for the current status of blacks, he placed the burden of advancement on his own people.

It was to be one of his last public statements. On February 26, 1975, just six days before the annual Savior's Day convention, Elijah Muhammad died of heart failure at Mercy Hospital in Chicago. He was 77 years old.

Because Muhammad had not written a will, his 19 legitimate and illegitimate children were forced to contend for his multimillion-dollar estate. The legal dispute was especially hard fought because his assets were estimated at $5.7 million.

Today the Black Muslims continue to flourish— although without Elijah Muhammad as their leader, the religious movement has splintered into different factions. Denouncing some of his father's philosophies, Muhammad's son Wallace formed a branch of the Nation that he opened to all races. Other new sects, such as the Ansaaru Allah and the Five Per Cent Nation, have chosen to emphasize the more mystical aspects of the movement. The ministry of Louis Farrakhan, the Nation's current leader, remains closest to the original precepts of the Messenger.

Since Muhammad's death, the Black Muslim movement has split into several factions. Louis Farrakhan (holding a Koran) is the current leader of the Nation of Islam, the sect that most closely adheres to Muhammad's original teachings.

For more than 40 years, Elijah Muhammad taught blacks to feel proud of their racial heritage. He carried out this mission by drawing on personal experience; he had, after all, forged his own identity through years of hardship and suffering. As James Baldwin put it shortly after meeting Muhammad at his Chicago home in the early 1960s, "The central quality of Elijah's face is pain, and his smile is a witness to it— pain so old and deep and black." ✿

CHRONOLOGY

1897   Born Elijah Poole on October 7 in Bolds Springs, Georgia

1903   Moves to Weona, Georgia

1911   Leaves school, after completing fifth grade, to work as a field hand and sawmill worker

1917   Marries Clara Evans on May 2

1921   First child, Emmanuel, is born

1922   Poole begins working for the Southern Railroad Company in Macon, Georgia

1923   Moves to Detroit; works at the American Can Factory and Chevrolet Motor Company; joins the Universal Negro Improvement Association (UNIA)

1930   Meets Wallace Fard, founder of the Black Muslim movement

1931   Joins the Nation of Islam and changes name to Elijah Muhammad; becomes close associate and friend of Fard's

1933   Appointed chief minister and head of Temple Number One in Detroit; takes charge of movement's administrative functions; moves family to Chicago

1934   Fard disappears mysteriously; Muhammad founds the Temple People

1935   Begins to travel throughout the United States, spreading the teachings of the Black Muslim movement

1941   Refuses to register for the military draft

1942   Arrested on May 8 for failing to register for the draft; receives a five-year sentence and is sent to Federal Correctional Institution at Milan, Michigan

1946   Wins release from prison and returns to Chicago to head the Nation of Islam

1948   Welcomes Malcolm X into the Nation of Islam

1962   Appoints Malcolm X national minister of the Nation; buys winter home in Phoenix

1963   Rift with Malcolm X grows

1964   Muhammad brands Malcolm X a traitor

1965   Malcolm X is assassinated

1972   Muhammad's wife, Clara, dies on August 12; Muhammad retreats into isolation

1975   Dies on February 26 in Chicago

FURTHER READING

Alexander, E. Curtis. *Elijah Muhammad on African American Education*. New York: ECA Associates, 1981.

Cushmeer, Bernard. *This is the One: Messenger Elijah Muhammad, We Need Not Look for Another*. Phoenix: Truth Publications, 1971.

Edmonds, I. G. *Islam*. New York: Watts, 1977.

Essien-Udom, Essien Udosen. *Black Nationalism*. Chicago: University of Chicago Press, 1962.

Goldman, Peter. *The Death and Life of Malcolm X*. Champaign: University of Illinois Press, 1979.

Haley, Alex, and Malcolm X. *The Autobiography of Malcolm X*. New York: Ballantine, 1964.

Haskins, James, and Kathleen Benson. *The 60s Reader*. New York: Viking, 1988.

Hobley, Leonard F. *Moslems and Islam*. United Kingdom: Wayland, 1979.

Lincoln, C. Eric. *The Black Muslims in America*. Boston: Beacon Press, 1973.

Marable, Manning. *Race, Reform and Rebellion: The Second Reconstruction in Black America, 1945–1982*. Jackson: University Press of Mississippi, 1984.

Meier, August, and Elliott Rudwick. *From Plantation to Ghetto*. New York: Hill and Wang, 1966.

Muhammad, Elijah. *Message to the Black Man in America*. Philadelphia: Hakim's Publications, 1965.

Young, Henry J. *Major Black Religious Leaders Since 1940*. Nashville: Abingdon, 1979.

INDEX

PICTURE CREDITS

AP/Wide World Photos: pp. 2, 3, 10–11, 15, 30, 39, 51, 64, 80, 88, 94, 100, 102, 103, 104; Bettmann: pp. 16–17, 42, 56–57, 61; Chicago Historical Society: p. 34; Georgia Department of Archives and History: pp. 20, 24, 25; Photo by Robert L. Haggins: p. 70; Schomburg Center for Research in Black Culture, The New York Public Library, Astor, Lenox and Tilden Foundations, Photo by Austin Hansen: p. 75; Library of Congress: pp. 33, 44; Eve Arnold, Magnum Photos: pp. 48–49, 92; Middle Georgia Archives: pp. 18–19; Schomburg Center for Research in Black Culture, The New York Public Library, Astor, Lenox and Tilden Foundations: pp. 23, 26, 37, 46–47, 52, 78, 84–85; UPI/Bettmann: pp. 13, 14, 40, 66, 69, 72–73, 82–83, 87, 97, 98, 101

MALU HALASA is a graduate of Barnard College in New York City. She now resides in London, where she writes for a number of periodicals, including the *Record Mirror, Blues and Soul, Soul Underground,* and *Cut.*

NATHAN IRVIN HUGGINS is W.E.B. Du Bois Professor of History and Director of the W.E.B. Du Bois Institute for Afro-American Research at Harvard University. He previously taught at Columbia University. Professor Huggins is the author of numerous books, including *Black Odyssey: The Afro-American Ordeal in Slavery, The Harlem Renaissance,* and *Slave and Citizen: The Life of Frederick Douglass.*